ALCOHOL
101

ALCOHOL 101

AN OVERVIEW FOR TEENS

Margaret O. Hyde
and
John F. Setaro M.D.

Twenty-First Century Books
Brookfield, Connecticut

Library of Congress Cataloging-in-Publication Data

Hyde, Margaret O. (Margaret Oldroyd), 1917–
Alcohol 101 : an overview for teens / Margaret O. Hyde
and John F. Setaro.
p. cm.
Includes bibliographical references.
Summary: Discusses alcohol use in the United States,
including the physical effects, the origin of the drinking age,
societal mixed messages, and the sociological impacts.
ISBN 0-7613-1274-9 (lib. bdg.)
1. Teenagers—Alcohol use—United States—Juvenile litera-
ture.
2. Alcoholism—United States—Physiological aspects—
Juvenile literature. 3. Alcoholism—United States—
Prevention—
Juvenile literature. [1. Alcoholism.] I. Setaro, John F. II.
Title.
HV5135.H83 1999
362.292—dc21 99-17926 CIP

Published by Twenty-First Century Books
A Division of The Millbrook Press, Inc.
2 Old New Milford Road
Brookfield, Connecticut 06804
Visit us at our Web site
http://www.millbrookpress.com

5

CONTENTS

CHAPTER 1
ALCOHOL 101: SOME BASIC FACTS
9

CHAPTER 2
WHY DO WE DRINK IN THE FIRST PLACE?
MIXED MESSAGES
12

CHAPTER 3
WHAT WE DRINK:
A BRIEF TOUR OF BEVERAGE ALCOHOL
24

CHAPTER 4
WHY 21? THE DRINKING AGE
29

CHAPTER 5
OUR BODIES WHEN WE DRINK:
THE ANATOMY OF A HIGH
38

CHAPTER 6
WHO'S DRINKING? ALCOHOL FOR ALL AGES
49

CHAPTER 7
BINGE DRINKING: A SPECIAL TEEN PROBLEM
59

CHAPTER 8
HOW MUCH IS TOO MUCH? ALCOHOLISM
71

CHAPTER 9
WHO GETS HURT? A LOOK AT SOCIAL PROBLEMS
87

CHAPTER 10
DO YOU HAVE A DRINKING PROBLEM?
98

NOTES
105

SUGGESTED READING
115

GLOSSARY
116

FOR FURTHER INFORMATION
119

INDEX
123

ALCOHOL
101

Chapter 1

Alcohol 101: Some Basic Facts

Darryl says he doesn't drink. He has a few wine coolers every day, but he considers them the same as fruit juice. Mary says she is not a drinker. She just drinks beer, so she figures that doesn't count. For religious reasons, Mrs. Hale never drank. Now that she is 80 years old, her grandchildren have introduced her to daiquiris. She says they taste so good that they can't have much alcohol in them, so she drinks a few each day. Sean only drinks on Wednesdays and on weekends, but he drinks heavily on those days. However, since he does not drink every day, Sean thinks he does not have a problem with alcohol. All these drinkers are mistaken.

Many drinkers know very little about alcohol. They do know that they are living in a society where alcohol is a common beverage. Even though it is illegal for teens, about 8 million American teenagers consume alcohol every week and about a half million of them drink for the sole purpose of getting drunk.[1] Nearly 4 million young people suffer from alcohol dependence, accounting for one-fifth of all alcohol-dependent people.[2]

In America, alcohol has been called the drug of festivals and funerals. For the majority of people over the age of 21, drinking is commonly acceptable social behavior. For those who drink, alcohol plays a part from the christening party to the graduation party, from the wedding reception to the 60th anniversary celebration, and all the parties in between. Victories in the World Series, the Super Bowl, and many other athletic events are toasted with drinks, and in major victories, champagne is poured over the winners. Boats and submarines are christened with champagne. In addition to the good times, alcohol is used to mourn failures and losses in the hope that it will help people through the bad times. Unfortunately, this kind of drinking often makes matters worse. According to Professor Bert L. Valee, M.D., of Harvard University, alcohol is a substance primarily of relaxation, celebration, and tragically, mass destruction.[3]

• FROM NONDRINKERS TO ABUSERS •

Although it may seem that America is largely a drinking society, more than a third of adults do not drink and many of them have good reasons. They range from protecting their health, being familiar with alcoholism, having religious reasons, disliking the feeling of being out of control, disliking the taste, and/or being able to enjoy life fully without alcohol.

Most adults who do drink do not abuse alcohol, knowing that alcohol can be a dangerous drug. Some do not know this; some do not care. Alcohol abuse is one of the most important health problems facing America and the rest of the world. It contributes to 100,000 deaths annually in the United States, making it the third-leading cause of preventable deaths.[4] Alcohol causes more teen deaths than the use of all other drugs combined.

Alcohol abuse ranges from quiet, secret drinking to the noise of bawdy parties. In some neighborhoods, especially in large cities, taverns and liquor stores have attracted unruly crowds of drunks who dominate the landscape. People urinate in the streets, fall asleep in the alleys, and engage in fights and sexual encounters in public places. In such neighborhoods, many voters sign petitions to outlaw alcohol.[5]

Alcohol itself is neither good nor bad. How it affects the health and behavior of people who drink it is good or bad. While alcohol is present in widely different scenarios, many drinkers and nondrinkers are unaware of basic facts.

Ask a group of people to define booze, and you will probably get many different answers. Booze is defined in dictionaries as hard liquor, as any beverage containing ethyl alcohol, the kind people drink, or in some dictionaries as both. The same may be true of questions about beer, wine, and liquor.

Why Do We Drink in the First Place? Mixed Messages

Matt, 15 years old, walks into a bar and orders a drink for his friend. The bartender jokes with him about how to make his favorite drink. A lady joins Matt at the bar, and they chat about interactive games.

If Matt were in a real bar, this would not be happening because he is below the legal drinking age. But Matt is in a bar on his computer screen, where he was warned that the site was for age 21 and over. It is easy for him to pretend that he is over 21.

Cele admires the girls in the vodka ads in her favorite magazine. They look glamorous, but she knows they did not get that way by drinking. Cele has done a project on the effects of alcohol, and she knows that vodka, other liquor, beer, and wine can give you bad skin, indigestion, bad breath, and added pounds, and can release inhibitions that protect you from dangerous behavior.

• CONFUSING MESSAGES FROM THE MEDIA •

Messages about alcohol come from a wide variety of sources, and they are confusing. Most of the messages that teens get from magazines, billboards, and sporting events link alcohol with attractive qualities such as happiness, prestige, athletic ability, sexual fulfillment, creativity, and success. They do not show how the abuse of alcohol diminishes and destroys these qualities.

Television programs and movies often portray drinking in a positive vein, too. The characters who drink are usually shown as glamorous, have successful careers, and seldom show any ill effects from drinking even though they pour themselves frequent drinks.

Now and then, public-service announcements and special educational programs on television promote responsible drinking, but more needs to be done to combat the large amount of underage drinking by people who hear only part of the story. Ads make it appear that everybody drinks, and that alcohol will make you more appealing to others. They never note that too much alcohol can make a person an object of humor, ridicule, or disgust.

• CONFUSING MESSAGES IN REAL LIFE •

There are confusing messages about alcohol in the real world, too. Many people who say they disapprove of heavy drinking consume more alcohol than they realize. However, many college students believe that binge drinking is more widespread than it really is. Even the term "alcoholism" has many meanings for different people.

Surveys to learn about young people's drinking habits, access to, knowledge of, and attitudes toward alcohol, yielded some surprising answers.[1] Students who believed many of the messages they heard were frequently misinformed. Some gave the following reasons why beer is the favorite beverage among teens: "It is cheap, easy to get, tastes good, and does not get you drunk as fast as other alcoholic beverages."[2] Part of this is true, but one 12-ounce (360-milliliter) bottle of beer contains the same amount of alcohol as a 5-ounce (150-milliliter) glass of wine or 1.5 ounces (45 milliliters) of hard liquor, the common standard for one drink. One can get drunk just as fast with beer.

Many young people don't seem to get the message about the legal drinking age. In one survey reported by the U.S. Department of Education, 5.6 million students nationwide were unsure of the legal age to purchase alcohol, and an estimated 1.6 million did not even know that such a law existed.[3]

About 96 percent of the students in a survey did not believe that a teenager could become an alcoholic, and about 87 percent did not know that a person can die from an overdose of alcohol. More than half believed that wine coolers do not contain alcohol.[4] Obviously, many of these students were getting the wrong messages.

• MESSAGES FROM PARENTS •

Even messages from parents can be confusing. Among many adults, a wide difference exists between their beliefs and their actions. Some parents send negative messages about alcohol because they drink so much that they do not know what their sons and daughters are doing.

Many parents who drink, and some who do not, are very strict about enforcing zero tolerance for those under the age of 21. Congress, in 1995, approved legislation that would require the federal Department of Transportation to withhold highway funds from states that do not enact zero-tolerance laws for underage drinkers who drive. Laws were enacted in many states so that licenses can be revoked when minors are discovered driving with a blood alcohol concentration (BAC) as low as 0.02 percent. For most people this is the equivalent of one glass of wine or one beer. This message has been spread among teens, resulting in a sharp drop in alcohol-related accidents.

Not everyone agrees that zero tolerance should always apply to those who are not driving, but some authorities follow the letter of the law. For example, in the spring of 1998, a group of 7th and 8th grade students who were studying French went to Paris where they tasted a thimbleful of wine as part of an elaborate three-hour dinner. When they returned home, the school principal, who had chaperoned the students, was banished to a teaching job in another district school. The school policy of zero tolerance extended to the use of any amount of alcohol in a school-sanctioned activity.

Controversies exist among parents and other adults about the messages they send to young people on the best way to teach them about alcohol. Many parents, however, agree with Dwight Heath, an anthropology professor at Brown University who studies drinking habits around the world. He suggests that drinking small amounts at dinner with adults is the best way for young people to learn about drinking. He believes that this deglamorizes and demystifies drinking.[5] But others fear that this approach encourages drinking.

Some parents think that the laws about underage drinking are wrong and help their teens break them by supplying beer for their parties. Parents have even called liquor stores complaining to salesclerks who would not sell kegs of beer for their teens' parties.

According to the Connecticut Coalition to Stop Underage Drinking, some parents who buy alcohol for their teenagers believe that they will drink anyway so they might as well drink at home. It may be true that if they drink at home, they will not have to drive, but many experts say that supplying beer for teens gives them the message that parents approve of underage drinking.

Parents who drink responsibly can send a strong message to their children. Many parents engage in conversations that help them deal with myths and peer pressure. For example, it is not true that everybody is drinking. It is true that drinking is an activity for adults, but it won't turn a minor into an adult. Only time and experience will do that.

Many parents are able to help their children understand that the social skills involved in making friends do not depend on alcohol. Teens who drink to feel more sociable often do things that they are embarrassed about later. Young people who like to stay in control welcome messages and rules from parents that help them withstand peer pressure.

Some parents are not concerned about discussing underage drinking with their own teens and children because they think they are not doing it. "Not my kid" is a belief that makes it easy for parents to let someone else worry about the problem, but many of them seem to be wearing blinders.

While public perception is that only troubled teenagers are heavily involved in drinking, counselors commonly see athletes and honor students with problems that arise from drinking and might have been prevented with parental guidance.

• AVAILABILITY OF ALCOHOL •

The huge amount of available alcohol sends its own message. It creates an environment suggesting that alcohol consumption and overconsumption are normal activities. Researchers have found that the amount of alcohol consumed depends partly on availability.

A person over 21 is the most frequent source of alcoholic beverages for underage drinkers, but many young people report that it is easy to buy beer in a local minimart, grocery, convenience, or liquor store. In some cases, store employees sell to them without even asking for identification (ID) cards, and in other cases, they accept fake IDs. A number of sting operations have been conducted by lawmakers and community activists in which young people are sent to stores to buy beer just to see if they can. Periodic "stings" demonstrate that laws are routinely violated. Penalties that result from these tests appear to have deterred some merchants from selling to minors.

In an effort to discourage underage drinking, a number of states have enacted laws to prevent the practice of ordering alcoholic beverages over the Internet and through newspapers and magazines. Industry spokesmen for the beverage industry claim that a teen will not go to the trouble of getting a credit card, ordering some wine, and waiting two weeks for it to be delivered. According to the Alcohol Epidemiology Program of the School of Public Health at the University of Minnesota, there are two options for regulating home delivery. Communities can prohibit the delivery of alcohol to residential addresses or place restrictions on home deliveries. Enacting the laws to curtail this mail-order industry grossing a billion dollars a year is reportedly easier than enforcing them.[6]

• ALCOHOL ADVERTISING •

Web surfers of all ages enjoy numerous ads for beer, wine, and liquor on the Internet. One features the Bud Ice penguin, who joined the frogs and lizards made famous in commercials for Budweiser beer. Like the trio of frogs that croak "BUD-WEIZ-ER" in various patterns until they form the brand name, and "Louie" and "Walter," the two animated lizards that challenge the frogs, the penguins are hip and with-it, active and social.

Ben, 12 years old, surfs the Web for alcohol ads, spends hours playing games, sending free postcards, and getting information about alcoholic beverages. He says the ads are fun and look cool. Ben associates them with good feelings, and he collects gear with alcohol brand labels. The web-sites include a warning that they are just for adults over 21, but Ben has no trouble making up an age that gives him access. Ben and perhaps millions of other young people watch alcohol advertising that is being used to form a relationship between view-ers and a brand name.

Ben has been watching alcohol-related online sites for several years. Many of the sites, like much of the advertising on the Web sites, tend to blur the lines between information, advertising, and mar-ket research.

The Center for Media Education (CME), an organization that monitors online advertising, found that brand icons dot the landscape of alco-hol advertising on the Web. It disclosed also that chat lines can be laced with promotional messages, market surveys can be disguised as games, and stories often carry subtle sales pitches. Many young viewers may find it difficult to distinguish the hype from the hip.[7]

Major alcohol beverage companies are a grow-ing commercial presence on the Web, with more than 35 brands represented.[8] CME also found that some hard-liquor and beer companies using the Web appear to be snaring teens and younger chil-dren looking for games, articles, and clothing. CME is concerned that the advertising techniques developing on the Web could have grave conse-quences for those who care about health issues, particularly in the area of alcohol and tobacco marketing.[9]

Will the cartoon ads and other advertising on the Internet and television that appears to be especially youth-oriented predispose boys and girls to drinking at an early age? Many factors are involved, but according to some experts, "The frogs are croaking and ... kids are drinking."

TV ads often reach millions of teens and children with messages that appeal to their humor, sense of fantasy, and identification with sports and glamorous, young-adult activities.[10] Cartoon and animal ads for beer have become youth favorites, even for those as young as nine. In one study, 200 children aged 9 to 11 were shown still, color images of characters from TV, including a picture of the Budweiser frogs. They were asked to recall the slogan associated with the pictured character(s) and the product advertised. Of these children, 81 percent identified beer as the product promoted by the frogs. They were better able to recall the frogs' slogan than the slogans associated with other characters, including Tony the Tiger, Smoky the Bear, and the Mighty Morphin Power Rangers. Girls were more accurate in recalling the Bugs Bunny slogan than the frog slogan, but boys were equal on their recognition.[11]

If children recognize the beer that the frogs, lizards and penguins advertise, do the ads encourage kids to drink it? According to George Hacker, director of the Alcohol Policies Project of the National Center on Addiction and Substance Abuse (CASA), "Brewers use animals, cartoons and superheroes to persuade impressionable young minds that drinking is fun, cool and without consequence."[12]

According to the Center for Science in the Public Interest, "Television advertising for alcoholic beverages affects the manner, style, and meanings of drinking in our society. It defines drinking as a positive and normative behavior. . . . Kids learn how, where, and why to drink from the ads."[13] Most people who watch television are aware of the large number of beer commercials. Karolyn Nunnallee, national president of Mothers Against Drunk Driving, says that the average U.S. child will view approximately 75,000 beer ads by age 18.[14]

According to the Center on Alcohol Advertising, grassroots activists won't quit until brewers stop child-friendly beer ads. Some activists are working to remove beverages with special appeal from the market. For example, the introduction of Phat Boy Malt Liquor caused an action alert among many youth advocates and community activists. According to the *Unofficial Rap Dictionary*, the word phat means "great or addictive," or "pretty hot and tempting." Advertising for Phat Boy claims that it is designed for the "next generation of malt liquor drinkers." The Marin Institute, an organization dedicated to drug and alcohol prevention, called for its recall through a petition to the company that markets this malt liquor.[15]

For 60 years, hard-liquor commercials were kept from radio, and for 48 years they were kept from television. When the Distilled Spirits Council of the United States (DISCUS) revised its code of practice in November 1996 to allow members to advertise in the broadcast media, it brought action.[16] A petition from more than 240 health, consumer, religious, and safety organizations was submitted to the Federal Trade Commission requesting an inquiry into the effects of broadcast ads. In addition to this action, many community activists and politicians are calling for laws to ban liquor advertising. The mission of the Center on Alcohol Advertising is to reduce children's exposure to advertising. This center enables communities to join a national movement by working locally.

Many teens are joining adults in working to restrict beer advertising that appeals to the young and in actions opposing broadcast commercials for liquor. Early in 1998, Michigan State University revealed the results of a poll that showed an overwhelming majority of public-television viewers would support strict rules on liquor ads. Half the participants surveyed said they believed that liquor companies that advertise on television are trying to influence teenagers to consume their products.[17]

Many of the public are in favor of counter ads, ads that would honestly reflect some of the risks and problems caused by alcohol. For example, one might state that alcohol is a factor in the three leading causes of death among youngsters 15 to 24 years old in America today: accidents, homicides, and suicides. Another might show the number of alcohol-related automobile accidents. Another might point out that as little as two beers or drinks can impair coordination and thinking.

While responsible drinking remains acceptable to most adults, new forces are at work in many communities to reduce the amount and kind of advertising of alcohol that influences underage drinkers. Young people are helping by telling advocates when, where, and how they are exposed to alcohol promotions. More and more people across the nation are becoming involved with local initiatives to curtail alcohol promotions that give the wrong message to children.[18]

Chapter 3

WHAT WE DRINK: A BRIEF TOUR OF BEVERAGE ALCOHOL

Beverage alcohol is ethyl alcohol, the least poisonous kind. It is a clear, colorless liquid that is given distinctive color and flavor from the things added to it or liquids used to dilute it when it is produced.

All beverage alcohol starts with the same natural process—fermentation. This is the natural decomposition of organic materials containing carbohydrates and the conversion of the sugars in them into ethyl alcohol.

Fermentation takes place naturally whenever the ingredients, carbohydrates and yeast, are combined in a liquid. Beer, wine, and liquor all begin with fermentation.

• BEER •

Beer is a beverage usually made from barley, hops, yeast, and water. (Other carbohydrates, such as wheat, oats, corn, rice, or rye may substitute for the barley.) The grains are sprouted, dried, and transformed into malt, then the malt is mixed with water, producing mash. The mash is cooked, and the liquid is filtered out of it. Hops, the flowers or cones from hop vines, are added for flavor. Then the mixture is boiled for a few hours, and yeast is added to begin the process of fermentation in which the starch in the mixture changes to alcohol.

When yeast encounters food, such as grains, honey, fruits, berries, and potatoes, it converts the sugar in them into carbon dioxide and alcohol. The yeast continues to a point at which, one might say, it dies of acute alcohol intoxication, and the fermentation process ceases.

This is a simplified description of brewing beer, a process that is quite complex. Just small variations in timing and ingredients can mean major changes in the finished product. Even changes in the composition of the water make a difference.

Beers have different flavor, body, aroma, color, and price. Beer comes in different styles. Ales, the heavier beers of old, are produced in a wide range of flavors and styles, such as porter, stout, pale ales, brown ales, and wheat beers. Lagers include most of the lighter mass-produced beers of today. And they, too, are in a wide variety of styles. Malt liquor is really a beer that has a relatively high alcohol content by weight, usually 5 to 8 percent, with some varieties reaching as high as 9 percent. Hybrid beers don't fit into the category of ales or lager. Specialty beers are brewed to a classic style of ales or lager but have some new flavor added. These may be made from unusual foods that are fermented.

Thousands of varieties of beer are produced in countries around the world. While these beers vary in ingredients, most contain between 3 and 6 percent alcohol. There are low-alcohol beers, which contain about half the alcohol of regular brews, and light beers, which contain fewer calories. Stout, porter, and other heavier beers have a slightly higher alcohol content.

Brewing beer takes a lot of equipment, work, and skill, but drinking it is easy and widespread. Beer is usually the first alcoholic beverage that is tasted. Junior and senior high-school students drink 1.1 billion cans and bottles of beer a year.[1] Many of them who say, "It's just beer," don't know that one can or bottle of beer equals a 5-ounce (150-milliliter) glass of wine or 1.5 ounces (45 milliliters) of liquor. They don't know that a six-pack can make them legally drunk drivers, and even a small amount can diminish driving skills.

• WINE AND WINE COOLERS •

Wine is the fermented juice of grapes, but the term "wine" is often used for fermented drinks that are made with various fruits and vegetables. For example, hard (or alcoholic) apple cider is sometimes called apple wine; perry is made from pears. Elderberry, blackberry, and dandelion wines are a few others that are not made from grapes.

The color of wine is determined by the color of the grapes from which it is made. Red wine comes from dark grapes, and white wine comes from white (green) grapes or dark grapes from which the skins have been removed. Rose or pink wine is usually classed as red. There are numerous varieties of color, taste, and aroma and a wide range in quality.

Wine-making is a delicate art, and the quality of the grapes from which wine is made is an important factor. The amount of alcohol in wine is usually between 7 and 14 percent. Fortified wines, such as sherry, Madeira, and port have an alcoholic strength of 18 to 20 percent. In order to fortify, or increase, the amount of alcohol in these wines, alcohol is added at the end of the fermentation process. As mentioned earlier, fermentation stops naturally at the point where the yeast can no longer live in the increased concentration of alcohol. With the added alcohol, some sugar is left unfermented, and the wine is very sweet.

Expensive sparkling wines are sometimes made by adding extra sugar and yeast to the wine after it is bottled. This causes a second fermentation with the production of hopped gases. Less expensive sparkling wines are made by forcing carbon dioxide in wine that has been cooled. Some sparkling wines are Asti Spumante, sparkling Moselle, sparkling Burgundy, and the "king of wines," champagne.

Wine coolers usually are cheap wines that are flavored so they taste somewhat like sodas, and they are popular drinks among students. About 42 percent of students who drink chose wine coolers when asked about their favorite drink.[2] Teens choose them because they taste good, are fruity, and do not have a strong taste of alcohol, and many think they do not have a high content of alcohol. Actually, wine coolers contain 6 percent alcohol, while regular beer contains 4 percent.[3]

• DISTILLED SPIRITS (HARD LIQUOR) •

Although yeast produces alcohol, it can tolerate concentrations of only about 16 percent. Distilling the liquid raises the level of alcohol. When any mixture of alcohol and water is boiled, more of its volatile alcohol goes into the vapor than remains in the water. When the vapor is condensed, it contains a much higher level of alcohol than the starting liquid.

Distilled spirits (liquors) include a wide variety of alcoholic beverages that have larger amounts of alcohol than beer and wine, but they are usually drunk in smaller amounts. Straight and blended whiskey (including Scotch, bourbon, rye, and Irish whiskey), gin, rum, and vodka are examples of distilled spirits. The alcohol in them is measured by proof instead of percentage. In the United States, 100 proof means 50 percent alcohol by volume. On the whole, whiskeys are 86 percent proof, gins are between 80 and 94 percent proof, and rum and brandy are usually 80 percent proof. All of them are made in different ways and classified according to certain qualifications.

While the liquors previously mentioned are usually consumed before a meal, brandies, which are made from fruits, are sweet after-dinner drinks. Cordials and liqueurs have a minimum of 2.5 percent sugar by weight.

• No Matter What You Drink •

How much you drink is far more important than what you drink. Understanding some basic information about the kinds of alcoholic beverages may help you to know what is going on in the world of drinkers and in making decisions when you reach drinking age.

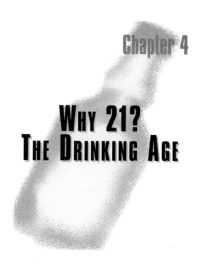

Chapter 4

WHY 21?
THE DRINKING AGE

T eenagers at 18 can vote and be drafted, so why can't they buy and drink beer? Old man Jones is drunk every night, while 19-year-old Tim helps at the homeless shelter for two hours every day and then has one beer. What old man Jones does is legal. What Tim does is not. Does this make any sense?

Even authorities do not agree about the drinking age, but they point out that ages of initiation vary and are thought to take into account the requirements, risks, and benefits of each act. One may vote at 18, drink at 21, rent a car at 25, and run for president at age 35.

Many 18-year-olds feel that they have a right to drink under John Stuart Mill's conception of liberty, which claims that the government should not intervene in actions we take that hurt only ourselves. Others argue that drunken teenagers are more likely than their seniors to launch themselves at other cars on a highway in a two-ton projectile going 90 miles (145 kilometers) per hour. Roadway accidents are the number-one cause of death among teens.[1]

• A Billion Beers a Year •

In a world that seems awash in alcohol, the age at which one is permitted to drink and at which millions of young people actually begin to drink varies widely. Even though alcohol is illegal in the United States for those under twenty-one, most people are aware that alcohol use among the young is very common. According to the Department of Health and Human Services, young people in the United States consume about a billion cans and bottles of beer per year.[2]

Counting the number of underage drinkers is difficult, because the definition for drinking varies. Many "drinkers" may be those who just have wine or champagne to celebrate a wedding or another special occasion with families at dinner. Some may be kids who have an occasional beer at a party, while others are binge drinkers.

A binge drinker is a person who consumes five or more drinks at one sitting, or by another definition, uncontrolled drinking for two days. About 4.4 million people below the age of twenty-one are binge drinkers, and 1.7 million are heavy drinkers, according to the Center for Substance Abuse Prevention (CASP).[3]

Today, many adults are greatly concerned about the extent of drinking among the young. Some are shocked to learn that the median age at which kids start to drink has been reported as 13.[4] Estimates of the total amount of alcohol consumed by college students each year is 430 million gallons

(1.6 billion liters), enough for every college and university in the United States to fill an Olympic-size swimming pool.[5] Most college students are under the legal drinking age.

• CHILDREN THROUGH THE YEARS •

Drinking at an early age is not new. For most of history there were no laws that established a drinking age. Before water was safe to drink, beer was both food and drink for people of all ages. Unborn babies have been, and still are, exposed to alcohol by mothers who drank regularly. Many parents have put beer in bottles to calm babies and fed it to their children for nourishment. Children in Europe, prior to the seventeenth century, commonly drank beer, and, according to one source, they consumed as much as 1 gallon (3 liters) of beer a day.[6] Beverages of earlier societies may have had much lower alcohol content than they do today.

• EARLY LAWS •

The laws under which young people could drink varied from state to state after the repeal of Prohibition in 1932. When liquor was available to 18-year-olds in New York State but the drinking age was 21' in nearby states, some teens would drive across the border for an evening of drinking and drive home while drunk.

In the early 1970s, many young people complained because their states had laws that made them old enough to go to war and to vote but not old enough to drink legally. Many 18-year-olds were sent to Vietnam to fight for their country. Across the nation there was a general movement toward greater rights and freedom for the young. A constitutional amendment was passed allowing 18-year-olds to vote. About 30 states lowered the age at which people could buy alcoholic beverages.[7]

The lowering of the legal drinking age was followed by an increase in fatal accidents. State motor-vehicle data from the 48 continental states found that lowering the drinking age for beer from 21 to 18 resulted in an 11 percent increase in fatalities among that age group.[8] The 1978 National Study of Adolescent Drinking Behavior found that 10th to 12th graders in states with lower drinking ages drank significantly more, were drunk more often, and were less likely to abstain from alcohol.[9] This and other reports increased concern about the number of drunk drivers causing tragic traffic accidents and about other drinking problems among the young, and brought pressure to raise the drinking age.

• RAISING THE DRINKING AGE •

In 1984, Congress passed an act to encourage each state to enact a minimum legal purchase age of 21 for alcoholic beverages by the year 1986. Such state laws were required by the federal government as a condition of receiving federal highway-construction funds.

Some critics argue that the high drinking age actually increases drunk driving by pushing underage drinking out of the bar and into the automobiles. However, statistics show a 55 percent drop in alcohol-related fatal auto crashes for 16- to 20-year-olds in the decade from 1984 to 1994, saving about 1,000 lives a year.[10]

• THE CONTROVERSY •

Today, opinions vary on whether the age at which alcohol can legally be purchased and consumed should be lowered, but most favor keeping the minimum at 21. Almost all agree that the law is widely broken.

Prohibition for young people under the age of 21 is not working, but is it better than legal drinking at a younger age? According to Professor Ruth C. Engs of Indiana University, the majority of college students under 21 consume alcohol in an irresponsible manner because it is seen as "forbidden fruit," a "badge of rebellion against authority," and a symbol of "adulthood." She notes that the decrease in drinking and driving problems are the result of many factors. Increased seat-belt and airbag use, education concerning drunk driving, safer automobiles, lower speed limits, and designated driver programs are among the factors that have played a part.[11]

Although the per capita consumption of alcohol and motor-vehicle crashes have decreased, abusive drinking behavior among the young has increased. Professor Engs suggests the need for alternative approaches to the problem. She notes that Italians, Greeks, Chinese, and Jews have relatively few drinking-related problems. These groups tend to share common characteristics. Young people learn to drink at home with their parents in a responsible manner, irresponsible behavior is never tolerated, and alcohol is not seen as a magic potion or a poison. Professor Engs suggests that changes should be made to teach responsible drinking and change our current unworkable prohibition.[12]

Many authorities who have studied the problem of abusive drinking among young people disagree with Professor Engs. They think lowering the minimum drinking age is a bad idea. In response to the point that lowering the drinking age will reduce the allure of "forbidden fruit," critics say that lowering the age will make alcohol more available to an even younger population, replacing "forbidden fruit" with "low hanging fruit."[13]

Not everyone agrees with Professor Engs on the point that children who consume alcohol at a younger age will learn to drink responsibly. Some claim that countries with lower drinking ages suffer from alcohol-related problems similar to those in the United States.[14]

In a survey of college administrators and security chiefs on enforcing the minimum drinking-age laws, most officials anticipated a host of negative consequences if enforcement of the age-21 limit were lessened. They felt there would be more student drinking, a drop in the college's image, parental displeasure, and a decline in academic work.[15]

Jim Hall, chairman of the National Transportation Safety Board, says, "State age-21 laws are one of the most effective public policies ever implemented to the Nation. . . . I am chagrined to report that some supposedly responsible officials would like to repeal them."[16]

Findings show that the 21 minimum drinking-age law has generally decreased the number of arrests called DUI (driving under the influence), youth suicides, marijuana use, crime, and alcohol consumption by youth.[17]

The behavior of 18-year-olds is particularly influential on the 15- to 17-year-old, as young people typically imitate the practices of those who are slightly older rather than of those who are significantly older. Therefore, if 18-year-olds can legally drink, their immediate, younger peers will drink, too.[18] Opponents of this idea claim that the teens in a younger age group drink heavily anyhow.

• SOME NEW RESEARCH ON DRINKING •

A report from the National Institute of Alcohol Abuse and Alcoholism adds new evidence to substantiate that underage drinking is a serious problem that can jeopardize health and lifetime prospects. The report indicates that the younger the age of drinking onset, the greater the chance that an individual at some point will develop an alcohol disorder.[19] According to the study, children who start drinking before the age of 15 were four times more likely to become alcoholics compared with those who waited until age 21.

Dr. Enoch Gordis, director of the National Institute of Alcohol Abuse and Alcoholism (NIAAA), claims that a 13-year-old with a family history of alcohol problems who has started to drink has a 58 percent risk of becoming an alcoholic. With no family history of alcohol abuse, the 13-year-old has a 28 percent chance. For those who start drinking at age 21, there is only a 10 percent chance of ever having a drinking problem.[20] However, one might ask if the early experiences "cause" alcoholism, or whether there was a tendency to begin with and these people simply start earlier.

• YOUNG DRINKERS AND TOLERANCE •

In the spring of 1998 a study by the Duke University Medical Center concluded that adolescents build a tolerance for alcohol faster than adults.[21] This may help explain why teenagers are more likely to drink themselves to death.

How alcohol affects the brains of young people is a subject under investigation. It is known that the brain does not finish developing until a person is about 20 years old, and one of the last regions to mature is involved with the ability to plan and make complex judgments. Animal studies show that young brains are more vulnerable to some of the dangerous effects of alcohol. If this is true for humans, adolescents who drink may be impairing brain functions used for memory and learning.[22]

• TEENS LOOK AT THE PROBLEM IN DIFFERENT WAYS •

While many teens are drinking before the legal age, many others are not complaining about the 21-year drinking law. Underage drinking is such a problem that many young people are joining the trend to put alcohol in a class with smoking. Many of them are targeting the heavy drinkers for social ostracism.[23] Some have even suggested that the drinking age be lowered to 16 or 17 as in some European countries and the driving age be raised so that people can learn to drink before they learn to drive. Although this is not a popular idea, many teens agree that something needs to be done about the drinking problem.

Chapter 5

OUR BODIES WHEN WE DRINK: THE ANATOMY OF A HIGH

"The alcohol went straight to my head," is a common expression among people who drink more than they intend. Of course, they probably know that the alcohol they drank went to their stomachs first. But they may not know that about 20 percent of it was absorbed through the stomach, and the remaining 80 percent went into the bloodstream by way of the small intestines. From there, the bloodstream carried it to virtually all the organs.

Alcohol is not broken down into other molecules the way food is. It is absorbed directly into the bloodstream as alcohol soon after it enters the body and is transported to all parts of the body. It reaches every part of the body, including the heart, brain, and liver.

Alcohol first affects the most complex area of the brain, the frontal lobe, which controls higher functions such as judgment and social inhibitions. It alters sensations and perceptions, emotions, motor skills, and sexuality. Small doses of alcohol may lead to sexual activity by overcoming inhibitions, but even moderate doses can spoil the capacity to perform and respond. Decreased levels of testosterone (male hormone) have been measured in young males after as few as four 12-ounce (360-milliliter) beers.[1]

Alcohol irritates the esophagus and other organs of the digestive system and interferes with sleep patterns and the functioning of many body organs, but most individuals can tolerate one standard drink per hour with no significant impairment.

• How Fast, How Much? •

The speed with which alcohol enters the bloodstream and goes to the brain depends on a number of factors. Generally, it takes about 15 to 20 minutes for alcohol to reach the brain.

Obviously, if one drinks fast, alcohol gets to the brain faster than if one sips or "nurses" the drink. Body weight plays a part, with a muscular person having a lower concentration of blood alcohol than a small person taking the same drink. For example, 4 ounces (120 milliliters) of whiskey in a 200-pound (90-kilogram) man will result in about half the blood alcohol concentration of a man who weighs 100 pounds (45 kilograms). However, the extra weight only slows the elimination of alcohol, so he would retain it longer.

• Different Effects for Different People •

Men and women differ in their processing of alcohol. Twins Caitlin and Leo weigh the same, but

Caitlin's body has a greater ratio of fat to muscle than her brother. Her body has proportionately less water than his. Because alcohol mixes with body water, a given amount of alcohol becomes more concentrated in a woman's body than in a man's. If both have the same number of drinks before dinner, Mary feels the effect more than Leo does. Her body absorbs about 30 percent more alcohol than his.[2] According to Charles Schwarzbeck of the University of Washington Medical School, the neurological systems of girls are more responsive to specific amounts of alcohol compared with boys. Even after adjusting for body weight, girls have higher levels of alcohol than boys when they drink the same amount of alcohol.[3]

Food slows the rate of absorption of alcohol in the bloodstream. Some people tend to empty their stomachs faster than others, so they feel the effect of alcohol more rapidly. When someone drinks on an empty stomach, the blood absorbs alcohol very rapidly. Peak alcohol concentration could be as much as three times greater in someone with an empty stomach than in someone who has just eaten.[4]

Jed, who never ate breakfast, carried vodka to school in his backpack rather than his lunch. He hid the bottle in the toilet tank before going to his first class. After the second period, he rushed to the bathroom, gulped down a large amount of vodka and passed out. The rapid absorption of a high concentration of alcohol suppressed the breathing centers of his brain. A classmate who found him on the bathroom floor called 911, and medics revived him on the way to the hospital.

People who play drinking games, take Jell-O shots (vodka and gelatin cubes), or consume large amounts of alcohol in a short time in other ways can develop serious medical problems.[5] Young people who cannot buy alcohol legally often drink quickly before leaving for an event. Then they cannot think as well or drive as well as they would if they drank the same amount slowly.

Anyone who has a long history of drinking can usually handle more alcohol than normal without feeling the effects. When someone is said to hold his liquor well, it may mean that tolerance to alcohol has developed, and large amounts of alcohol are needed to produce a high.

Although beer, wine, wine coolers, and liquor contain the same kind of alcohol, the addition of other ingredients, called congeners, that give flavor to the alcohol, and the addition of mixers affect the rate at which alcohol is absorbed. When alcohol is mixed with carbonated beverages the rate of absorption is increased, while mixing it with water slows the rate.

• ELIMINATING ALCOHOL FROM YOUR BODY •

Your body treats alcohol like a poison and starts to get rid of it immediately. About 5 percent of the alcohol in your bloodstream is exhaled through your lungs, and excreted through sweat, saliva, and your urine. Alcohol breath is the result of the part that you exhale, and this is the basis for the test that measures how much a driver has been drinking.

The liver removes the rest of the alcohol from the blood by a process known as oxidation. First, an enzyme breaks it down into acetaldehyde, a toxic chemical that can make a person feel sick if it accumulates in the body. When you drink small amounts of alcohol, acetaldehyde is broken down rapidly before nausea occurs. The alcohol becomes water and carbon dioxide. Heavy drinkers appear to "hold their liquor" because they have upgraded liver enzymes and therefore can process more alcohol.

Metabolism, the breaking down of alcohol into other substances, proceeds at a constant rate in the liver. One ounce of alcohol is oxidized per hour. If you drink more than this amount, excess alcohol continues to circulate in your blood, passing through your brain and other organs again and again until the liver has had a chance to metabolize it.[6] The extra alcohol accumulates as it waits its turn for metabolism, and results in higher concentrations of blood alcohol and intoxication.

Hangovers are the result of drinking heavily over a short period of time. The headache, nausea, and shakiness of a hangover begin about 8 to 12 hours later. These reactions are due partly to the body's withdrawal from alcohol and partly to poisoning by alcohol and other components of the drink. Time is the only cure.

• DIFFERENT EFFECTS •

Alcohol affects people in many different ways, and can affect the same person in different ways at different times. The main factors that determine how alcohol affects you are: the amount you drink, your weight, how much you have eaten, your mood, your sex, and your drinking habits.

Generally, low doses increase pleasure, self-confidence, and sociability. They calm, relax, and reduce tension. But they also lower inhibitions, impair concentration, slow reflexes, impair reaction time, and reduce coordination. After the first half-hour, the euphoric feelings are usually replaced by drowsiness, making drinkers quiet and withdrawn. This pattern often results in people having another drink in order to sustain the initial feelings.[7]

In someone who is depressed, lonely, or suicidal, the depressant effects of alcohol can deepen these feelings. For other drinkers, verbal and physical aggressiveness is increased. An angry person may become angrier. About 3 million violent crimes occur each year in which victims perceive the offender to have been drinking at the time of the offense.[8]

People who drink regularly and become tolerant to the effects of alcohol may be able to drink more than others before appearing intoxicated. They may continue to work and socialize reasonably well, but their bodies deteriorate. Their drinking problem may not be recognized until severe damage develops, or until they are hospitalized for other reasons and suddenly experience serious withdrawal symptoms because the supply of alcohol to their bodies has stopped.

• SOCIAL DRINKERS AND POSSIBLE BENEFITS •

A social drinker is usually defined as someone who drinks regularly but does not get drunk and does not crave alcohol. Molly's mother drinks a glass of wine each evening with her dinner. Her father drinks 2 ounces (60 milliliters) of bourbon before dinner. Neither one drinks more than this, with the exception of an occasional extra drink at a party. They are social drinkers and are unlikely to develop into chronic alcoholics.

Both of Molly's parents are careful not to increase the amount they drink. Their doctor has suggested that small amounts of alcohol can benefit their health. According to several studies, women who have one drink a day and men who have two drinks a day are less likely to develop heart disease than people who do not drink any alcohol or who drink larger amounts.[9] As mentioned earlier, one drink equals one 12-ounce (360-milliliter) bottle of beer or wine cooler, one 5-ounce (150-milliliter) glass of wine, or 1.5 ounces (45 milliliters) of 80 proof distilled spirits. Small amounts of alcohol, especially wine, may help protect against coronary heart disease by reducing stress, by raising levels of "good" HDL cholesterol, and by reducing the risk of blood clots in the coronary arteries.

While small amounts of alcohol may be healthy for your heart, even slightly larger amounts per day significantly increase your risk of dying from heart disease, stroke, or cancer and may lead to the development of high blood pressure. Women who drink are at greater risk of breast cancer. The benefit of a drink per day varies according to age and the underlying risk of cardiovascular disease. The benefit appears to be largely confined to those over 60 years of age who are at increased risk.[10]

Doctors do not recommend that nondrinkers start drinking in order to benefit their hearts. There is always the danger that drinking may get out of control, and people can protect themselves against heart disease by low-fat diets and exercise.[11]

• MIXING ALCOHOL WITH MEDICINES •

Even with moderate drinking, alcohol can react with some prescription medications, leading to increased risk of illness, injury, or death. It is estimated that alcohol-medication interactions may be a factor in at least 25 percent of all emergency-room admissions.[12]

Alcohol can cause problems with medications in several ways. First, alcohol behaves similarly to medications in the body, so their effect may be lessened. But in some cases, a single drink, or several drinks over several hours, may inhibit a drug's metabolism by competing for the same set of enzymes. This increases the availability of the medicine, thus increasing the patient's risk of harmful side effects. Third, enzymes activated by chronic alcohol consumption transform some drugs into toxic chemicals that can damage the liver and other organs. Fourth, alcohol can magnify the effects of sedative and narcotic drugs at the sites of action in the brain.[13]

If you drink while taking certain antibiotics to treat diseases, you may suffer from nausea, vomiting, headaches, and possibly convulsions. Alcohol increases the effect of some antidepressants, impairing driving skills. A chemical called tryamine, found in some beers and wine, interacts with some antidepressants to produce a dangerous rise in blood pressure. As little as one standard drink may create a risk that this interaction will occur.[14]

ALCOHOL AND PRESCRIPTION DRUGS

ALCOHOL COMBINED WITH...	CAN CAUSE...
Sleeping medications (e.g., *Halcion, Dalmane*) Tranquilizers (e.g., *Xanax, Valium, Ativan*) Anti-depressants (e.g., *Elavil, Tofranil*) Pain relievers (e.g., *Percodan*, codeine) Some muscle relaxants (e.g., *Robaxin, Soma*) Antihistamines (e.g., *Chlor-Trimeton, Benadryl*) Motion-sickness pills (e.g., *Dramamine*) Allergy medications (e.g., *Contac, Dristan*) Some cough/cold products Some high-blood-pressure medications (e.g., *Aldomet*)	Excessive drowsiness, impaired coordination, mental confusion, rapid intoxication, loss of consciousness, impaired breathing. Can be fatal.
Anti-anginal medication (e.g., *Isordil*, nitroglycerin) Some high-blood-pressure medications (e.g., *Minipress, Apresoline*, diuretics	Dizziness, fainting, lightheadedness, loss of consciousness, falls that could result in physical injury.
Aspirin Anti-arthritic medications (e.g., *Feldene, Naprosym*, ibuprofen) Potassium tablets Blood thinners (e.g., *Coumadin*)	Increase in stomach irritation, possible increase in stomach bleeding.
Flagyl Oral anti-diabetic medications (e.g., *Orinase*) Some anti-fungal and antibiotics agents (e.g., *Chloromycetin*)	Can cause *Antabuse*-like reaction (weakness, headache, nausea/vomiting, flushing, rapid heartbeat, difficulty breathing.)
Blood thinners (e.g., *Coumadin*) Anti-diabetic medications (e.g., *Micronase,* insulin) Epilepsy medication (e.g., *Dilantin*) Gout medication (e.g., *Zyloprim*)	Interference with control of certain medical conditions (diabetes, epilepsy, gout). Can cause change in effectiveness of drug treatment.

Justin was taking Dilantin, a drug to prevent epileptic seizures that had been a problem for him in the past. One evening, some of Justin's friends persuaded him to join in toasting the winning soccer team. Justin was having a wonderful time, drinking toast after toast, until he suffered a seizure. He had been free of seizures since he had begun taking his medicine. After that experience, he toasted the team's future successes with alcohol-free tonic water.

Narcotic pain relievers and alcohol can be a dangerous combination since both are "downers." One case that made many people more aware of this possibility was that of Karen Ann Quinlan, who apparently combined alcohol and Darvon in 1975. She lapsed into a coma that lasted ten years until her death in 1985.[15] Even a single drink can significantly increase the sedative effects of Darvon.[16]

Nonprescription pain relievers can have some less obvious effects when combined with alcohol. Aspirin and some other pain relievers can cause stomach bleeding and prevent the way that blood clots normally. These risks can be increased with alcohol, particularly among those who abuse alcohol or drink heavily.

The following warning label appears on Tylenol (acetaminophen) bottles: "ALCOHOL WARNING: For this and all other pain relievers, including aspirin, ibuprofen (Advil), ketoprofen (Actron and Orudis KT), and naproxen sodium (Aleve), if you generally consume 3 or more alcohol-containing drinks per day you should consult your physician for advice on when and how to take pain relievers." Chronic alcohol use can activate enzymes that transform acetaminophen (Tylenol and others) into chemicals that can cause liver damage.[17] Alcohol and some other pain relievers may cause stomach and intestinal bleeding.[18]

Alcoholic beverages have the potential to cause problems when combined with about 100 different prescription and over-the-counter medicines. According to Dr. Enoch Gordis, director of the National Institute on Alcohol Abuse Addiction, even very small doses of alcohol probably should not be used with antihistamines and other medicines with sedative effects.[19]

Heavy drinking that was once romanticized as daring and sophisticated is now considered a health hazard. Some of the effects of heavy drinking are discussed in the next chapter.

Chapter 6

WHO'S DRINKING?
ALCOHOL FOR ALL AGES

• THE COSTS: HUMAN AND FINANCIAL •

Sara was born impaired because her mother drank alcohol while pregnant. Harold lost his job driving a truck, and his health insurance along with it, because he was spending most of his time in the hospital because his stomach was bleeding. Angela, a mother of three teenagers, drank secretly but heavily: She suffered incurable liver damage and, after five months in intensive care, died waiting for a liver transplant that never came. Jerrold went into the hospital for knee surgery, but he did not tell his doctors about his habit of consuming eight beers per day at home. In the hospital he was deprived of alcohol, and he went into withdrawal. This had serious complications, which quadrupled the length of his hospital stay. Arthur retired from his job at age 70 but cannot enjoy his retirement. His heavy vodka habit caused brain damage, which gradually became so serious that he had to be placed in an institution under state financial support. These stories illustrate the human and financial costs of alcohol addiction.

• FETAL ALCOHOL SYNDROME •

Whether because of shame, guilt, or anxiety, Sara's mother was unable or unwilling to recall how much alcohol she drank while pregnant. When doctors found that many of Sara's physical and intellectual problems were like those of a baby with fetal alcohol syndrome (FAS), her mother and father admitted to some earlier binge drinking. The child's head and body size were small for her age, her facial features were abnormally formed, and her ability to learn new things was clearly delayed compared with other children. Saddest of all, these characteristics would remain with Sara through adolescence and beyond, and she would never be able to escape the tragic, though fully preventable, circumstances of her birth.[1] What was worse, at age 16, troubled and socially isolated, she began drinking alcohol herself, raising the specter of yet another generation damaged by FAS.

Although observers a century ago saw that alcoholic mothers produced children with significant mental and physical deficiencies,[2] the first scientific report defining FAS was published in 1968.[3] Because of mounting evidence linking alcohol use in mothers to fetal abnormalities, the U.S. government in 1981 advised against drinking alcohol in pregnancy. Today, all alcoholic beverages sold in the United States carry the familiar written warning: "According to the Surgeon General, women should not drink alcoholic beverages during pregnancy because of the risk of birth defects." Nevertheless, 15 percent of pregnant women in the United States were consuming alcohol in a 1995 survey.[4] Although light or social drinkers may be influenced by public-health campaigns, there is concern that mothers who are alcoholics may not be reached or affected by these messages. One problem is that many alcoholics exist in social isolation. Another concern is that many people may be confused by what they read and hear about the possible benefits of alcohol for the circulatory system. Even if these reports are true for men and older women, such findings certainly do not apply to pregnant women.

FAS is now the most commonly known cause of mental retardation in the United States, with between 5,000 and 10,000 affected children born each year, or one in 500 to 1,000 live births. In women who are chronic alcoholics, the rate of producing FAS children is 2.5 percent or more, and a newborn baby with an FAS brother or sister has 100 to 400 times the chance of having FAS herself.[5] It is not exactly clear how much intake of alcohol is necessary to cause FAS, although some studies show that up to 45 percent of women taking 3 ounces (90 milliliters) of alcohol per day will have a child with full-blown FAS. Two drinks per day will cause some weight loss and intellectual difficulties.

More important, no one knows if any amount at all is safe, and perhaps large individual doses (binge drinking) may be the worst of all, particularly at the early stages of pregnancy. Since it appears that no level of exposure is good, women should quit drinking alcohol as soon as they know they are pregnant. After her child is born, a woman may pass alcohol to the infant through breast milk.[6] Staying alcohol-free during breast-feeding is probably a good idea as well.

The effects of alcohol on the growing fetus are widespread, leading scientists to propose that alcohol damages the fundamental building blocks of life. Many different areas of development are affected, and in some cases they include critical malformations of brain structure.[7]

Doctors can diagnose FAS based on the history of alcohol use in the mother and the child's small size in comparison with age, facial abnormalities, and problems in the central nervous system. Although many cases of FAS are severe, there are degrees of seriousness, probably based on the actual timing and dose of the mother's alcohol intake. Heavy alcohol exposure during early pregnancy, when vital organs take shape, might be expected to cause a more severe case of FAS. The facial deformities are seen at birth or early in childhood. FAS children have small heads, small eyes with drooping eyelids, short noses with a low bridge, and thin upper lips. The pair of vertical ridges connecting nose and mouth are often completely absent, and the ears are low, and the chin is receding. Computers can help to create a standard model of the facial features of FAS children so that new cases can be identified more easily.

FAS children may have seizures at birth because of alcohol withdrawal. As infants, they sleep poorly, have abnormal reflexes, short attention spans, impaired speech development, and have trouble learning colors, words, and how to tell time. FAS children often remain thin because they do not eat well. They may also have physical abnormalities of the heart, joints, and urinary system. Their average IQ is less than 70, and older adolescents with FAS fare poorly in school, achieving math and word skill scores on a 2nd to 4th grade level. Learning and intelligence difficulties may become lifelong problems.[8]

FAS adolescents show poor social judgment and have multiple behavioral problems. In a Washington, D.C., medical clinic specializing in FAS children, the most frequent reasons for referral for special kinds of care were conduct disorders, including extreme anger, and learning disabilities.[9] Teenagers with FAS can become socially isolated, depressed, and may engage in criminal or high-risk sexual behavior. Later, they may grow up to become alcoholics themselves.

The treatment for FAS children, as for others who have delays in development, consists of patience, care, and specialized training. The most severely affected FAS children may need treatment in an institutional setting, especially since their alcoholic parents may be unable to cope with such a challenging child-raising situation. There is a trend toward legal prosecution of mothers who are exposing a fetus to harmful drugs or alcohol. Such laws and judicial rulings indicate the seriousness of society's concern over the future health of its children. Yet it is possible that such legal safeguards may have the opposite effect by driving troubled mothers away from seeking help because they fear being reported to law-enforcement authorities. This issue is not yet resolved. Since there is no cure, the best approach for fetal alcohol syndrome is prevention.

As the examples in this chapter show, the use of alcohol across months or years can damage many of the systems of the body. The brain and central nervous system, the digestive system, the blood-forming organs, and the heart and circulation can all suffer the ravages of alcoholism.

The human brain becomes habituated to alcohol for reasons that are not completely clear. But withdrawal from alcohol can provoke jitteriness and seizures ("rum fits") or major episodes of delirium tremens (DTs). Symptoms can start eight hours after the last drink, and reach a peak at 24 hours. Hallucinations, seeing things that aren't there, are frequent. The most severe form of DTs involves hyperactivity, fast pulse, high blood pressure, fever, and dilated pupils. Patients must be hospitalized and treated with sedative drugs. In spite of treatment, the death rate from DTs is still 10–15 percent, probably because patients injure themselves, experience heart attacks or strokes related to the extreme physical stress, or develop pneumonia after inhaling food or saliva while they are disturbed.

Many chronic drinkers have difficulty sleeping and spend less time in the important phase known as REM (rapid eye movement). Confusion, psychosis (not knowing what is real), and difficulties in problem solving, memory, and thinking may develop. Many long-term alcoholics may become demented. Alcohol may exert much of its effects by altering the brain's chemical messengers. Older alcoholics frequently have atrophy, or loss of brain tissue, on imaging studies such as CAT scans. The cerebellum, the part of the brain that governs balance, is highly sensitive to alcohol. Major users of alcohol can develop severe walking difficulties. Chronic drinkers of red wine can destroy the connection between the right and left halves of the brain, called the corpus callosum. Nerves in the arms and legs can suffer as well. In a condition known as polyneuropathy, alcoholics complain of burning feet and loss of feeling.

Poor nourishment among chronic users of alcohol brings about major vitamin deficiencies. When alcoholics lack thiamine, a B-vitamin, they may develop a disease called Wernicke's encephalopathy. These alcoholics show abnormal eye motion, walking difficulties, and mental confusion. A further extension of this disease in severe cases is called Korsakoff's psychosis, where patients have an extreme disorder of memory. They cannot remember any newly introduced information, so to compensate for absent memory they create fictitious responses, in order to satisfy the questioner. These disorders can respond to vitamin treatment and proper nutrition.

Alcohol in excess attacks the liver, the major body organ that breaks down toxic substances. An enzyme, or protein, in the liver changes alcohol into water and carbon dioxide. Toxic by-products can contribute to liver damage. The liver can accumulate fat and start to function poorly. Alcohol can cause the liver to become inflamed, a painful condition called alcoholic hepatitis.

Late-stage alcoholic liver disease causes cirrhosis, a hardening and shrinking of liver tissue. Cirrhosis can lead to the congestion of bile, a greenish brown fluid that helps in the digestion of fat, and jaundice (deep yellow color of skin and whites of eyes), as well as liver cancer. With cirrhosis, other essential liver functions like blood clotting and digestion begin to fail, and blood can back up into bulging veins in the stomach and esophagus. These vessels may burst, leading to massive bleeding and death. In the United States alcoholic cirrhosis of the liver causes 25,000 deaths each year. A liver transplant may be lifesaving, but many surgeons are reluctant to perform the operation in an alcoholic patient because of the possibility of continued alcohol use. Cancers of the esophagus, throat, and mouth have been linked to alcohol use as well. Alcohol ingestion can cause stomach irritation (alcoholic gastritis) as well as ulcers of the stomach and small intestine, which cause vomiting and bleeding. The pancreas, another producer of digestive juices, can become severely inflamed by alcohol, in some cases fatally.

Anemia, or low content of red blood cells in the bloodstream, may be a consequence of the toxic action of alcohol on the bone marrow where new blood cells are produced. Lack of clotting factors, based on alcoholic liver damage, can cause abnormal bleeding anywhere in the body. A small amount of alcohol on a daily basis (average of one drink) may protect the heart against cholesterol vessel blockages and may lower blood pressure slightly, but heavy drinking of alcohol is harmful to the circulatory system. The irritating effect of alcohol in high concentration can lead to serious disturbances in the heart rhythm (holiday heart syndrome), and long-term use can poison the heart muscle and make it too weak to pump efficiently. Too much alcohol can raise blood pressure, and can even produce bleeding brain strokes (cerebral hemorrhage).

• ALCOHOLISM AND THE ELDERLY •

With the large number of serious medical problems that can arise from alcoholism, it is interesting to consider the characteristics of alcoholic persons who somehow survive to reach old age. Very little is understood about this group of people. In the over-65 age group, by strict criteria alcoholics are estimated to make up 5–10 percent of patients who are part of the medical system of clinics, doctors' offices, or hospitals. They may constitute 2–4 percent of the general community of elderly persons, although some authorities believe that estimate is too low.[10] Dr. M. Carrington Reid of the Yale School of Medicine and the West Haven Veterans Affairs Medical Center specializes in the problem of alcoholism among the elderly. He says that much more work needs to be done in this field. Measurement of actual consumption is difficult, because recall and memory are unreliable guides. It is not clear whether current or past cumulative consumption of alcohol is more important, or who is really an alcoholic in this age group.

Dr. Reid has observed that as patients get older they self-regulate their alcohol use in a downward direction. Whether this happens because of worsening vision, impaired balance, or deteriorating ability of the liver to process alcohol is not yet known. As a result, researchers may need to construct a new scale of tolerable doses of alcohol based on age. Once the size and nature of the problem are defined better, age-appropriate treatments can be developed. Older alcoholic patients do not like to participate in group programs, for instance, because they feel that the other participants are too young. Clearly alcoholism is a problem for people of all ages.

Chapter 7

Binge Drinking:
A Special Teen Problem

Janel, a freshman who has been at college just a few weeks, has been enjoying the social life at some of the fraternity houses. This Sunday morning, as she walks slowly toward her dorm, she is bleary-eyed and confused. She tries to remember exactly what happened at the party last night. Did she have unprotected sex? Would she be HIV positive? Might she be pregnant?

The grass near the row of fraternity houses is strewn with beer cans, plastic cups, and empty bottles. A nearby kiosk has a sign advertising pitchers of beer for a dollar on Monday nights at the nearby tavern. Another sign announces a meeting of V-8, a new organization of students who are tired of the mess the binge drinkers are making. They are not asking for abstinence, just responsible drinking.[1]

Janel is just one of the freshmen who came to college thinking that binge drinking was expected of everyone who wanted to be popular. Janel still believes that almost everyone drinks heavily on weekends. She does not know that she is one of the many students who perceive their peers' drinking levels to be higher than their own and higher than they actually are.[2]

It is true that binge drinking is widespread. Binge drinking is often defined as having five or more drinks in a row in the preceding two weeks, but it is also defined as uncontrolled drinking for two days.[3] Binge drinking was reported by 30.4 percent of high-school seniors, 24.8 percent of 10th graders, and 15.6 percent of 8th graders in 1996.[4]

In 1998 the Harvard School of Public Health College Alcohol Study, which surveyed students at 116 universities and colleges across the country, reported that 42.7 percent were binge drinkers. This was only a slight decrease from the 44.1 percent reported in the landmark 1993 study by the same group.[5] The small drop was attributed to an increase in students who do not drink at all. Significantly more students abstained from drinking in 1998 (19 percent), up from 15.6 percent in 1993. According to Dr. Henry Wechsler, the principal investigator in the Harvard study, this may be due to alcohol education efforts or that abstainers are repulsed by the binge-drinking way of life.

According to the 1998 Harvard report, drinkers experienced more alcohol-related problems that affected their health, education, safety, and interpersonal relations than in the 1993 report. These included driving after drinking, damaging property, getting injured, and falling behind in schoolwork.[6]

Although the amount of binge drinking can make it seem that "everyone does it," a careful look at the figures shows this is not true. The binge drinkers make the headlines. Dangerous drinking begins to subside after the age of 22, according to Lloyd Johnston, a University of Michigan researcher.[7]

Young people of college age who do not attend school are less likely to be binge drinkers.[8] But the use of alcohol as a "head drug," drinking until one is intoxicated, is common among some teens and young adults in and out of school. For example, many construction workers stop at a local bar after work and encourage young apprentices to join them in their rounds of drinks. Young workers fear losing jobs if they do not keep up with their bosses, and many develop habits of heavy drinking. Sometimes, the job loss they were trying to avoid results from their alcohol abuse.

Binge drinking for a small percentage of students begins around the age of 13, tends to increase during adolescence, and peaks in young adulthood (ages 18-22), the college years, then gradually decreases. Half or more of college binge drinkers also binged in high school. They came to college expecting to drink heavily and find cheap alcohol available in large volume.[9]

• WHY BINGE? •

With the obvious ill effects of binge drinking, the question "Why binge?" is common. Some young people who drink heavily would answer the question with "Why not?" Teens tend to see themselves as immortal, so they do not concern themselves with the long-term health effects of drinking. Since they feel invincible, they are often willing to take part in risky activities that may have negative consequences. Janel's experience is just one example of this.

Other reasons for heavy drinking are many. Teens and young adults are in the process of establishing an identity apart from their parents, and a key element in this process is maintaining meaningful connections with a peer group. Utmost importance is attached to being accepted by that group. Alcohol eases socialization and lets the two sexes mingle with fewer inhibitions, even though the effects of heavy drinking often produce negative results. Where binge drinking is a part of the social life, many individuals do it just to feel accepted, not realizing that most students are not doing it.

Alcohol use may function as a psychological defense against feeling small and helpless.[10] Drinking supplies many young people with an illusion of being adult. It emulates adult behavior while simultaneously signaling rebellion against adult authority. All this takes place in a social climate in which some people value intoxication.[11]

• WHY NOT BINGE? •

Many young people who are supposed to be having a good time at a party where people binge are vomiting and passing out instead. Now and then a person dies of an overdose of alcohol. When this happens, even some of the drinkers take notice and wonder if it is time to make changes in their way of having fun. Still, an estimated 2.6 million students do not know that a person can die from an overdose of alcohol.[12]

While getting dead drunk can mean getting dead, most binge drinkers become unconscious before they reach this stage. However, when binge drinking results in death, many people show concern. Scott Krueger's death is an example of such a tragedy. In September 1997, this freshman at MIT (Massachusetts Institute of Technology) went to a party at the off-campus house of the fraternity he was pledging, or trying to enter as a member. He joined the celebration with his fraternity brothers by drinking until his blood level was five times the standard for drunken driving in the state of Massachusetts. He became comatose and never woke up.

Krueger's death came just weeks after a tragedy at Louisiana State University where Benjamin Wynne celebrated receiving his fraternity pledge pin and downed the equivalent of 24 drinks. Police found about two dozen men unconscious on the floor of his fraternity house that night. It was a fatal night for Benjamin Wynne. Although these tragedies received much media attention, they may be just the tip of the iceberg.

About 4,000 Americans die each year from alcohol poisoning, and some of them are college students.[13] While death is the most extreme consequence of heavy drinking, many other students in high school and college suffer from alcohol poisoning. The number of students who almost die or suffer serious health problems from heavy drinking is unknown, but it is probably quite large.

Among frequent binge drinkers, 62 percent of men and 49 percent of women admitted driving under the influence of alcohol.[14] Binge drinking can also lead to alcoholism, unsafe sex, date rape, and a long list of other emotional and physical problems.

• CONFRONTING BINGE DRINKING •

Changing the environment that supports heavy drinking is a challenge not only to parents and school authorities but also to many young people who are aware of some of the problems it causes. Although many students do not want to, or expect to, rid their schools of drinking, they hope to change the climate. Who needs binge drinking?

Heavy drinking plagues drinkers from high school through college, including nondrinkers who suffer, too. Nondrinkers and social drinkers report that bingers cause problems ranging from trashed campuses and interfering with their sleep to an increase in vandalism and the number of sexual assaults. For example, on the University of Delaware campus, most of the physical and sexual assaults, accidental injuries and fatalities, much of the property damage, and other disruptions are alcohol-related.[15] Most students want a healthy environment on campus, and many are working toward that goal.

One approach to combating high-risk drinking is destroying the myth that heavy drinking plays a paramount role in college life. Exaggerated perceptions of drinking by others causes some teens to try to keep up, and this feeds the binge-drinking epidemic. Many students routinely see messages that promote drinking in student newspapers, at sporting events and concerts, and in residence halls and cafeterias, making drinking seem more common than it really is.[16] At one college, students were asked to estimate the number of binge drinkers on campus. The actual percentage was published in the college newspaper before a poll was taken to see how accurate the estimates were. Most of the students overestimated the number. This positive peer-pressure approach is considered a viable method of fighting alcohol abuse on campus at many schools. Two dozen colleges in the United States are finding it helpful to spread the truth about the real amount of binge drinking.[17]

Janel, who sought help at the student-health center, moved to an alcohol-free dorm, a kind of dorm that is becoming popular at many schools. Some colleges have "wellness floors" where alcohol is prohibited. Here, some of the residents are especially interested in living without the loudness, late night guests, and vomit of drinkers; some have personal reasons, such as recovering from substance abuse; and some are interested in holistic living. At the University of Michigan, for example, 27 percent of those living on campus are in substance-free dorms. Colleges nationwide are climbing on the bandwagon.[18]

Much pressure to lower the amount of drinking at schools comes from students who have added their voices to efforts to change the drinking culture. Many schools, with the cooperation of students, have added a wide range of activities that are alcohol-free. Such activities range widely, from staging ice-cream parties and "mocktail" parties to peer-education programs. Alcohol-free nightclubs feature music, dancing, and comedy. Some schools, like Clark University in Worcester, Massachusetts, have turned campus pubs into coffeehouses.[19] Student groups and administrators work together to increase interest in theater groups, to limit the alcohol at parties, and to exclude ads from local bars in their newspapers. Some spread the word that alcohol abuse is not as common as most students think.

• FRATERNITIES •

It is common knowledge that underage drinking has long been a part of fraternity life. Fraternity parties and other "blasts" are famous for their drinking games in which players consume large amounts of alcohol. Some of these parties begin with "funneling," in which beer from a keg is shot into a drinker's mouth. Next comes a visit to a popular bar where there are drinkers' specials, such as "bladder busts," in which drinks are cheap until someone has to go to the bathroom. Ladder prices, where drinks are cheap before a certain time and increase in price as the evening wears on, encourage gulping and fast drinking. These and other friendly promotions, such as ads in school newspapers, promote heavy drinking.

Fraternity and sorority leaders are being recruited by school administrators and community activists to discourage heavy drinking, but many of these students have alcohol-related problems of their own.[20]

Deaths, lawsuits, and rising insurance premiums have had some effect on fraternities throughout the nation. In December 1997 the National Interfraternity Council passed a resolution recommending alcohol-free chapter houses. Many seek a return to the founding principles of fraternities, which call for scholarship and public service rather than bonding with peers just because of membership. Nationally, two fraternities have committed to having dry houses by the year 2000.[21]

Although many freshmen think they have to binge in order to get into a fraternity or eating club at college, this is not always the case. Fraternities have been taking various courses of action to discourage heavy drinking. Some groups, such as half the eating clubs (the equivalent of fraternities and sororities) at Princeton, have changed their method of selecting members. Rather than pledging sessions that include drinking, a lottery system is used, in which students name their preferred club choices and a computer makes the selection.[22]

Tagging beer kegs is becoming a common approach to slowing the flow of cheap beer at parties. In 1990, Greenfield, Massachusetts, began a keg registration program after a young person who had been drinking drowned. Such accidents and other serious problems that have followed keg parties have motivated many communities to introduce keg registration. In these programs, retailers are required to keep a record of the metal tag identification number, the purchaser's name, address, phone number, and driver's license number. A deposit is required, and this fee is lost if the keg is returned with the identification tag missing or defaced.

In December 1998 a pact by 24 Boston colleges set out a blueprint for action to curb the culture of drinking that pervades student life. Among other things, this was a statement of intent to encourage more first-year students to live in alcohol-free housing, to ban tailgating parties at athletic events, and prohibit alcohol at frat and sorority rush events.[23]

Sorority groups have urged fraternities to go alcohol-free. The National Panhellenic Conference, an umbrella organization for 26 national women's collegiate sororities, adopted a resolution supporting the efforts of several national men's undergraduate fraternities to ban alcohol from their residences and refocus fraternity life on education and good values. Just as smokers are frowned on in restaurants and offices, party animals in some fraternities are facing the threat of extinction.

• SADD AND BACCUS •

Approaches to curbing high-risk drinking come from many fronts. Two national organizations that attempt to discourage drinking are SADD and BACCUS. Caleb was active in his high-school chapter of SADD (Students Against Drunk Driving), a national organization that has thousands of chapters in high schools and also has a college program. (SADD changed its name to Students Against Destructive Decisions to expand its mission to other traffic-safety, drinking, and drug-use issues). Caleb continued to belong to

SADD in college and recruited other members from his dorm. Many were glad for the chance to have peer support in their refusals to drive drunk.

SADD calls on students to sign a pledge to parents and friends that they will not drive drunk or ride with a drunk driver. They suggest ways of accessing safe transportation home. In high school, Caleb knew he could contact his parents for help in a situation in which he would have been stranded unless he rode with a drunken friend. At college, he could call on someone in the group known as the Safe Ride Program.

BACCUS (Boost Alcohol Awareness Concerning University Students) is a national organization that seeks to foster peer-education programs that discourage driving drunk and misuse of alcohol.

• IN CASE A FRIEND NEEDS HELP •

In addition to calling 911 in case of emergency, there are several things you should know in order to help a friend who has had too much to drink:

1. Don't let the person drink more alcohol.

2. Don't let the friend drive, wander outside, become involved in sexual encounters, or any kind of risky behavior.

3. Put an unconscious person on his or her side to avoid choking if vomiting occurs.

4. If the person is unconscious, monitor breath, heart rate, and body temperature. If any of these is abnormal, call 911.

From individuals to major groups such as the United States Senate, there is awareness that the time has come for the culture of binge drinking by the young to change.

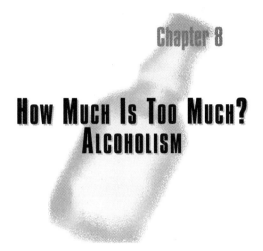

Chapter 8

How Much Is Too Much?
Alcoholism

Young people become alcoholics for many reasons. In addition to enjoying the good feelings
from the alcohol and being part of a peer group,
there are family and environmental influences, the
wish to appear grown-up or to rebel against
authority figures, a response to advertising, and
genetic predisposition. Usually, a combination of
these and other reasons are involved. Consider the
different stories of Sara, Gary, and Bartie.

• SARA •

Sara, 16 years old, received many awards for her
athletic achievements, and she seldom broke any
of the rules laid down by her strict parents. Now
and then she joined the crowd who spent much of
their free time drinking beer. She would not touch
the "hard stuff," and she was usually careful about
how much she drank. Sara said she didn't see any
harm in the way her friends drank. Most of them
did not get into trouble.

Sara and two of her friends began increasing the amount they drank. A few beers just didn't give them that great feeling any more, for they were developing a tolerance to the alcohol. Even when they each drank a six-pack every day, they did not think of themselves as having an alcohol problem.

• GARY •

Gary, a 19-year-old, drinks heavily and thinks he might be an alcoholic. His first drink was a bottle of beer, stolen from his family's refrigerator when he was 10. For the next few years, he and his friends met every Saturday for a few beers and a smoke. Gary liked drinking with kids a few years older, and the beer made him feel good.

By the time Gary was 13, he took gin and vodka from his father's liquor cabinet and poured water into the bottles so his father wouldn't notice that the level was going down. He considered trying the same trick with bourbon and Scotch but he was afraid his father would notice the difference in the color of the liquor. His father was an alcoholic who never noticed what Gary had done.

By the time Gary was in 10th grade, his drinking problem was getting him into big trouble. One night he went to a dance drunk and vomited on the floor in front of everybody. His friends began avoiding him, and his life was a mess. He drowned his sorrows with more liquor.

Gary missed classes part of each school day and spent much of his time with a bottle. He managed to squeak though high school by cheating on tests and charming teachers into passing him.

Although Gary knew he was brilliant, he did not realize that he was not very smart about his drinking habits.

Sometimes when Gary was drunk, he had unprotected sex. After he tested positive for HIV, he blamed the girl who gave it to him. He still refused to blame alcohol for any of his trouble. Actually, alcohol can alter an immune system and make a person more susceptible to acquiring HIV infection.

• BARTIE •

"My mother doesn't care if I drink now and then as long as I am not on drugs," says 17-year-old Bartie. She says everyone in her family drinks, but they do not use drugs. They are very strict about marijuana, but they do not consider alcohol a drug.

Bartie says there is not much to do in her neighborhood. She drinks when she is bored, and that is much of the time. Sometimes she wonders if she has an alcohol problem, but she is too busy planning for college to think much about it.

• TEN YEARS LATER •

When Sara became an alcoholic, she learned that her parents did not drink when she began to drink because they both had alcohol problems when they were younger. At the time they grew up, the stigma of alcoholism was so great that they did not tell anyone. Her parents hid their problems away in the closet of family history, where alcohol problems of other generations were hidden. Sara's parents thought they were protecting her by not telling her, but just the opposite was true. If they had warned her that she had a risk factor, she might have avoided drinking.

Sara, who now attends Alcoholics Anonymous (AA), is open about her problem. She tells her children that they have a four to five times greater risk of becoming alcoholics if they drink than if no one in their family suffered from the disease. Although alcoholism occurs in one out of six families in America, it is still often discussed in hushed tones. One of the greatest weapons against alcoholism is prevention. This means education.[1]

Gary died from AIDS about six years after he contracted HIV. Although his alcoholism would have been treatable, his AIDS was his primary medical problem, and the diseases that came with it played the major role in his death.

Bartie's binge drinking at college soon grew out of control. She was unable to keep up with her classes and left school for a rehabilitation program. After she stopped drinking she returned to school, and today she works as a school counselor who understands the problems of students who like to drink too much.

• WHAT IS ALCOHOLISM? •

Alcohol dependence, or alcoholism, is psychological and/or physical reliance on alcohol. The National Institute on Alcohol Abuse and Alcoholism (NIAAA) defines it as a disease that includes alcohol craving and continued drinking despite repeated alcohol-related problems, such as losing a job or getting into trouble with the law. Its four symptoms include:

1. Craving—a strong need or compulsion to drink
2. Impaired control—the inability to limit one's drinking on any given occasion
3. Physical dependence—withdrawal symptoms, such as nausea, sweating, shakiness, and anxiety when alcohol use is stopped after a period of heavy drinking
4. Tolerance—the need for increasing amounts of alcohol in order to feel its effects.

Not everyone agrees on the definition of alcoholism, but there is agreement about the difference between alcohol abuse and alcoholism, and both of these are in the title of the national institute mentioned above.

Alcohol abuse refers to patterns of abuse that give rise to health problems and/or social problems. Alcoholism also involves craving, or addiction. The body needs alcohol to function normally. Alcoholism afflicts about 13.7 million people in the United States. Fourteen percent of the population will become dependent on alcohol at one time in their lives.[2]

Alcoholism can ruin careers, health, marriages and whole families. Its effects on victims of car accidents and other innocent victims are far-reaching. It has little to do with what kind of alcohol a person drinks, how long one has been drinking, or even how much one consumes. It has a great deal to do with a person's uncontrollable need for alcohol.

An alcoholic is physically dependent on the drug, alcohol, and signs of withdrawal begin within hours after an alcoholic stops drinking. The symptoms, often referred to as the DTs (delirium tremens), include profound anxiety, tremors and sleep disturbances. In extreme cases, there can be hallucinations (often jokingly referred to as pink elephants) and seizures.

Withdrawal from alcohol dependence is no joke. The body's chemistry has been altered by alcohol, and it tries to restore its balance. Someone experiencing the symptoms of DTs should be taken to the emergency room of a hospital. Untreated, it can even cause death.

In the hospital, a person suffering from withdrawal is monitored for physical problems and anxiety, delusions, and hallucinations. The patient may be restrained to prevent self injury or injury to others. Sedatives and other medications may be given to prevent seizures. Delirium tremens usually lasts 1 to 5 days, but it can be as long as 10 days.

A hangover can be considered a mild withdrawal after an episode of heavy drinking, but its causes are not completely understood. Headaches and nausea are well-known symptoms. The common treatments—coffee, exercise, and cold showers—do not cure hangovers. Feeling better comes with rest and time for the body to return to a normal state after alcohol has been eliminated.

Withdrawal symptoms from alcoholism are much worse than hangovers. The action of the body in withdrawal is one reason that most experts consider that alcoholism is a disease. Like many other diseases, alcoholism follows a generally predictable course, has recognized symptoms, and is influenced by both genetic and environmental factors that are being increasingly well-defined.[3]

• THEORIES OF ALCOHOLISM •

Authorities who disagree with those who believe that alcoholism is a disease emphasize the importance of environmental influences, such as abuse, peer pressure, physical and emotional stress, in causing people to seek and become dependent on alcohol. They believe that alcoholics have developed a way of life in which they use drinking as a major strategy for coping with their problems. Some scientists who disagree with the disease concept believe that the focus of attention must shift from drinking per se to the meaning of drink for certain persons and the way of life in which its role has become central.[4] Certainly many young people use alcohol to deal with deep personal problems, but not all of them lose control over drinking.

While many theories may contribute to psychological therapy and social programs, alcoholism nevertheless is a progressive illness and can prove fatal if not treated. More and more, it has come to be viewed as a complex disease entity in its own right. Addiction can occur after three months or 30 years.[5] Whether you drink because of feelings of anxiety, depression, rebellion, loneliness, or just to have fun, it's what drinking does to you that counts.

• RISKS FOR ALCOHOLISM •

Almost everyone agrees that some people have a higher risk for alcoholism than others. One signal of possible risk is being able to "hold liquor better than most people," consuming more and not showing it. But when they reach a drunken state, it is more intense and causes more dysfunction.[6] Individuals who are at high risk for alcoholism may suffer blackouts, or memory lapses, after the first few times they drink.

The tendency toward alcoholism has a genetic component in many people. When a certain gene or genes are present, the use of alcohol is more likely to lead to alcoholism. It has been clear for many years that alcoholism runs in families. Studies of twins who were adopted separately at birth allowed researchers to evaluate the influences of heredity and environment. These studies strongly support genetics as a factor in alcoholism.

• ALCOHOLIC MICE •

Two strains of mice helped scientists to understand the connection between heredity, environment, and alcoholism. One strain of mice loved alcohol and would drink it rather than water, even when the concentration of the alcohol was as high as 70 percent. Another strain of mice hated alcohol and would choose water even when the concentration in the alcohol supply was as low as 0.02 percent.

Alcohol-hating mice that were tested under stress came to prefer increasingly strong doses of alcohol and became alcoholic mice. When other alcohol-hating mice were injected with high levels of alcohol, they also gradually came to prefer stronger and stronger doses of alcohol above water. When another group of alcohol-hating mice were deprived of vitamin B and some essential proteins, they too became alcoholic after several months. When the brains of mice from the different experiments were examined, all had approximately the same brain chemistry even though they were different to begin with. These experiments seem to indicate that no matter whether the brain chemistry was changed by heredity, environment, drugs, nutrition, or a combination of factors, the changes can all lead to addiction.[7] Of course, human beings are much more complicated than mice, but their brain chemistry can also be altered by heredity, environment, and alcohol use. People born with a low genetic or environmental susceptibility would take longer or larger amounts to become alcoholics if they ever reached that state.

• CHILDREN OF ALCOHOLICS •

Alcoholism has been called a family disease. If you have an alcoholic parent or grandparent, your chances of becoming an alcoholic, if you drink, are increased. Many young people avoid alcohol because they have seen what it has done do to their relatives. Some avoid it because they know that they are vulnerable to alcoholism.

Children of alcoholics usually grow up in very special circumstances. No one knows how many alcoholics in the United States are under the age of 18. Estimates vary from about 7 million[8] to 17.5 million.[9]

Ellen is only 11 years old, but she takes care of her family. Each day when she comes home from school, she leads her drunken mother to bed. Then she prepares dinner for her younger brother and sister. Sometimes her father helps, but many times he comes home from work and sits in front of the television drinking while she tends to the younger children. She has no time for friends and the usual activities of girls her age.

Dan is a teenager who is withdrawn. He does not ask friends to come to his house because he does not want anyone to see his mother beat his little brother when she is drunk. Many times she is asleep in the afternoon, but the house is always a mess. He would be embarrassed to have his friends see the way things are at home.

Dan feels a lot of guilt. His mother blames him because his father left one night after Dan disobeyed him. The disobedience had little to do with his father's leaving, but Dan does not know this. He thinks his mother's drinking is his fault, even though it is not.

Children of alcoholics often take on one or more of the following roles:

1. Model child, like Ellen;
2. Lost child, like Dan, who is unable to form close friendships and seems disconnected from emotions around him;
3. Mascot, or family clown, who minimizes serious issues but usually has superficial relationships with others, including members of his own family;
4. Problem child, who has personal problems. This child often begins drug and alcohol abuse early.

The National Association of Children of Alcoholics believes that no child of an alcoholic should grow up without support from counselors, physicians, educators, or other advocates. Many school-based and student-assistance programs work to meet the needs of children of alcoholics.

Another organization, the Children of Alcoholics Foundation, works with people who are helping children of alcoholics through numerous instructional materials for teachers, physicians, guidance counselors, mental-health specialists, and the general public. The foundation produces videos and other materials. One three-session program has several components, including "The Images Within: A Child's View of Parental Alcoholism." More information about these groups can be obtained by contacting them at addresses beginning on page 122.

Al-Ateen is an outgrowth of Al-Anon, a program for families of alcoholics that is based on the same principles as Alcoholics Anonymous. Meetings are free, anonymous, and confidential. Members learn ways to cope with their problems and encourage one another. They learn that they are not the cause of anyone else's drinking and can detach themselves emotionally from the drinker's problems while continuing to love the person.

• TREATMENT •

For those who become addicted to alcohol, the drug comes to assume more importance than work, family relationships, and physical health. Some alcoholics drink around the clock to avoid withdrawal symptoms.

Is Someone's Drinking Getting to You? Al-Ateen Is for You.

Al-Ateen is for young people whose lives have been affected by someone else's drinking. The following 20 questions may help you decide whether Al-Ateen is for you.

1. Do you have a parent, close friend, or relative whose drinking upsets you?
2. Do you cover up your real feelings by pretending that you don't care?
3. Are holidays and gatherings spoiled because of drinking?
4. Do you tell lies to cover up for some one else's drinking or what's happening in your home?
5. Do you stay out of the house as much as possible because you hate it there?
6. Are you afraid to upset someone for fear it will set off a drinking bout?
7. Do you feel nobody really loves you or cares what happens to you?
8. Are you afraid or embarrassed to bring your friends home?
9. Do you think the drinker's behavior is caused by you, other members of your family, friends, or rotten breaks in life?
10. Do you make threats, such as, "If you don't stop drinking, fighting, I'll run away?"

11. Do you make promises about behavior, such as, "I'll get better grades, go to church, or keep my room clean" in exchange for a promise that the fighting and drinking will stop?

12. Do you feel that if your mom or dad loved you, she or he would stop drinking?

13. Do you ever threaten or actually hurt yourself to scare your parents into saying, "I'm sorry," or "I love you"?

14. Do you believe that no one could possibly understand how you feel?

15. Do you have money problems because of someone else's drinking?

16. Are mealtimes frequently delayed because of the drinker?

17. Have you considered calling the police because of the drinker's abusive behavior?

18. Have you refused dates out of fear or anxiety?

19. Do you think your problems would be solved if the drinking stopped?

20. Do you treat people unjustly because you are angry at someone else for drinking too much?

If you answered yes to some of these questions, Al-Ateen may help you.

From "Is Someone's Drinking Getting to You?" copyright 1981, by Al-Anon Family Group Headquarters, Inc. Reprinted by permission of Al-Anon Family Group Headquarters, Inc.

As people become more aware of the genetic and environmental factors in the development of alcoholism as a disease, the social stigma is decreasing and families are hiding it less. Fewer consider it a moral weakness, so more alcoholics are no longer ashamed to ask for help. This means that more people enter treatment sooner.

There is controversy about how alcoholism should be treated, as well as disagreements about the reasons for it. Alcoholics Anonymous (AA) is a fellowship of men and women, including young adults, who share their experiences, strengths, and hopes with each other to stay sober and help others stay sober. There are approximately 51,000 chapters in the United States and 39,000 chapters overseas, with nearly 2 million members. AA is the most widespread program that helps alcoholics, and many alcoholics in other forms of treatment also attend AA. Each chapter is based on one alcoholic helping another and is run entirely by local membership, with anonymity and no charge. Anyone who wants to stop drinking may join. Today, this includes many young people.

The first chapter of Alcoholics Anonymous in a secondary school began in 1988 at Pacific Palisades High School in California after ten alcohol-related deaths in a ten-month period occurred.[10] Today there are many chapters for young people that meet in a variety of places. You can obtain information about a group near you in your phone book or by contacting AA at the address or Web site given on page 122. Meetings are held on the Web at http://stayingcyber.org.

Alcoholic Anonymous and many other treatment programs emphasize that alcoholism is a psychological condition, which requires therapy that seeks to understand the source of the cravings. Some specialists believe that alcoholics should be treated with counseling alone, while doctors insist that drugs are crucial tools. Each alcoholic is different and may need to try one or more approaches.

In addition to using medicines that help patients in withdrawal, doctors can prescribe several drugs that curb the urge to drink. The prescription drugs disulfiram (Antabuse) and naltrexone (ReVia) may have unpleasant or dangerous side effects. A new drug, acamprosate (Campral), that has been widely available in Europe is expected to help many Americans remain sober. The abnormal activity in the brain that is caused by alcoholism may last for a year after a person stops drinking, leaving the alcoholic prone to relapse. It is thought that acamprosate restores chemicals that carry messages between nerve cells in the brain to their normal condition.[11]

Many alcoholics relapse once or several times before being able to remain sober. Studies show that a minority of alcoholics remain sober one year after treatment, many take longer, while others are unable to stop drinking for any length of time. The longer one abstains from alcohol, the more likely one is to remain sober. Ongoing support of family and friends is important for recovery.

• HELPING AN ALCOHOLIC OBTAIN TREATMENT •

Alcoholism has been called a disease of denial. Elmo's brother Dan refused to admit that alcohol was creating serious problems for him and his family. His parents had always rescued him when he was in trouble, making excuses for him and paying for damages he caused while drunk. Elmo persuaded them to stop all "rescue missions" so that Dan would experience the problems his drinking caused and be more motivated to get treatment.

Elmo gathered information about local treatment options and discussed them with her parents. In a "family conference," which included Dan when he was sober, Dan accepted the fact that his drinking was a problem and that it was not due to a moral weakness. He was willing to try a meeting of Alcoholics Anonymous. Elmo offered to go with him.

Elmo helped her family to understand that they were not responsible for Dan's drinking and that they, too, would benefit from a support group such as Al-Anon.

Helping an alcoholic is a challenging situation. One does not have to wait for a crisis, or for the alcoholic to "hit bottom," before being supportive in getting help. However, an alcoholic cannot be forced to get treatment unless there has been a violent incident involving the police or a medical emergency. Remember, you and your family cannot make someone stop drinking. You can only be supportive of a person who is in treatment.

Chapter 9

WHO GETS HURT?
A LOOK AT SOCIAL PROBLEMS

I t is 6 P.M. on a dark December afternoon. Three girls leave the mall after shopping and take the elevator to the parking garage. Two boys step out of the shadows and demand their money. One boy, who is obviously drunk, beats the smallest girl with the handle of a gun until she is unconscious. When he is apprehended, the boy explains he drank because he wanted "liquid courage" for the robbery, but he did not plan to hurt anyone. Actually, the beer lowered his inhibitions. Alcohol weakens brain mechanisms that normally restrain impulsive behavior, including aggression.[1]

Alcohol is closely associated with many kinds of violent crimes, including murder, rape, assault, and child and spousal abuse.[2] Most people who drink do not become involved in dangerous behaviors, but studies show that alcohol seems to play a large role in crime. Among the 11.1 million victims of violence each year, 1 in 4 were certain that the offender had been drinking before the crime.[3]

According to one study, 60 percent of convicted homicide offenders drank just before they killed.[4] This does not mean that alcohol was the cause of the crime, but it appears to be a contributing factor.

While intoxication alone does not cause violence, alcohol-related homicide accounted for 11 percent of the 100,000 alcohol-related deaths in the United States in one year.[5] According to one study, almost 50 percent of murders are linked to excessive alcohol consumption.[6] Many young people who would not normally be involved in violent crime behave differently after drinking. Daphne Abdela, who reportedly had a drinking problem, was just 15 years old when she was involved in the murder of a man in New York's Central Park.[7] Another 15-year-old, Tommy Mullen, was found hanging by a belt from a second-floor banister after what appeared to be an alcohol-fueled game of "chicken." His family said there was little doubt that he drank to excess before it happened and being intoxicated may have crippled his judgment.[8] Stories similar to the above can be told of many young people who drank and played Russian roulette and other games that they would not have played when they were sober.

• PARTY TIME AND DANGEROUS BEHAVIORS •

Alcohol and fun don't always mix well. Spring breaks, holidays, and proms are especially notorious for alcohol-related accidents. Many students cooperate with authorities to provide alcohol-free travel to and from dances, and enjoy parties without drinking alcoholic beverages. Committees of parents, students, and teachers often cooperate to make party time safe and alcohol-free. In spite of this, some proms and other celebrations are the sites of drinking accidents. Alcohol poisoning and overdoses have already been discussed in the chapter on binge drinking.

Other kinds of alcohol-related dangerous behavior still accompany many celebrations. For example, during spring weekend at the University of Connecticut at Storrs in 1998, 80 people were arrested and thousands of dollars of damage to university property resulted from the melee.[9] The damage done by the heavy drinkers at celebrations reflects on the whole school's reputation even though only a small number of students were responsible for the riots.

• DRINKING AND DRIVING •

About 3 in every 10 Americans will be involved in an alcohol-related crash at some time in their lives, according to the National Highway Traffic Safety Administration.[10] This statistic usually concerns people when they read it, but many forget about it when they have to drive home after a few drinks at a party.

Alcohol and automobiles result in tragedy in many different ways. The girl who drove her car into a tree, the man who was driving in the wrong lane and killed three people in an oncoming car, the woman who hit a pedestrian and dragged her a thousand feet were all under the influence of alcohol. One boy climbed through the sunroof of a car on his way to a party, slipped from the roof, and fell to his death. He would probably not have done so if he had not been drinking heavily.

Year after year, many thousands of people are injured and killed on the highways. Alcohol-related traffic injuries are the leading cause of death among American teenagers.[11] Pedestrians, both sober and drunk, are also victims of car and motorcycle accidents.

Too often students lose a class member to drunken driving before graduation, and school commencements and yearbooks become memorials once again. Although alcohol-related fatalities for all age groups had been decreasing, 1996 figures show an increase in fatalities in the 15–20 age group since 1990.[12] There are more teens in the population today, but also more binge drinking.

Alcohol is a major factor in bicycle injuries and deaths, too.[13] Sue said she had only a few beers before she rode her bicycle in the path along the road, but her coordination was impaired. She did not feel drunk when she climbed on her bicycle, nor did she feel that her ability to ride a bike was affected when she veered onto the road and was struck by a car.

• "JUST A FEW BEERS" •

Even a few beers or small amounts of other kinds of alcohol can play a part in all kinds of driving accidents. The amount of alcohol in a person's blood can be easily tested with a Breathalyzer since some alcohol is removed from the body through the breath. The Breathalyzer measures the amount of alcohol per deciliter of blood, and results are known as blood alcohol concentration (BAC). Alcohol begins to affect driving ability and the likelihood of crash at blood alcohol concentrations as low as 0.02 percent.[14] Although the permissible BAC for driving varies in different states, most states consider 0.10 percent the legal limit.

The probability of a crash increases at any BAC above zero. It increases significantly at 0.05 percent and climbs rapidly after 0.08 percent. If you drive with someone who has a BAC above 0.15 on a weekend night, your likelihood of a being in a fatal single vehicle accident is 380 times greater than it is with a nondrinking driver.[15]

How can one tell if he or she reaches a BAC that is illegal to drive? If you are under 21, you are considered legally intoxicated by almost all states if your BAC is 0.02. This is known as a "zero tolerance law." With zero tolerance laws any amount of alcohol in the body of a young driver is an offense for which the driver's license can be suspended.

Charts such as the one on the following page show the blood alcohol concentration after drinking various amounts, but in real life many factors are involved. To be safe, don't drink and drive.

A driver who is intoxicated may not appear that way. However, he or she would have delayed reaction time and other problems that would make driving dangerous even in normal traffic conditions. A person is considered 20 times as likely to have a fatal accident when his or her BAC is 0.10 as when it is zero.

Many groups and individuals are working toward lowering the legal limit in all states, but some attempts at the federal level have failed. Lobbyists for liquor interests depicted the bill as an assault on harmless social drinking, while those who supported the bill suggested that anyone drinking enough to exceed a BAC of 0.08 might be

When to Say When

The amount one can drink before becoming impaired varies according to a number of factors. The chart shows levels of alcohol in the blood depending on sex, weight, number of drinks, and how fast they are consumed. Levels over 0.08 grams of alcohol per 10 liters of blood—the limit being considered by the Federal Government—are shaded.

One shot of distilled spirits, a glass of wine, or 12 ounces of beer contain about the same amount of alcohol

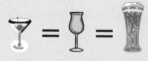

WOMEN								
Weight in pounds	115			145			175		
Number of drinks	2	4	6	2	4	6	2	4	6
Time in hours	1	2	3	1	2	3	1	2	3
BLOOD ALCOHOL CONTENT	0.06	0.12	0.19	0.05	0.09	0.14	0.04	0.07	0.11

MEN								
Weight in pounds	160			190			220		
Number of drinks	2	4	6	2	4	6	2	4	6
Time in hours	1	2	3	1	2	3	1	2	3
BLOOD ALCOHOL CONTENT	0.03	0.06	0.09	0.02	0.05	0.07	0.02	0.04	0.05

Source: Department of Transportation

considered unsafe on the road. The legal limit in many countries is much lower than it is in the United States. In Sweden it is 0.02, and in many other countries it is 0.05.[16]

Many factors are involved in a person's ability to drive while under the influence of alcohol, but no one argues that drinking before driving decreases the ability to make good decisions, slows reaction time, impairs judgment and coordination, and makes steering and speed control more difficult. No wonder people say, "Friends don't let friends drive drunk." Binge drinking, four or five drinks in an hour, means drunk.

A number of organizations that are concerned with drinking and driving continue to focus on young people. Remove Intoxicated Drivers (RID) is a national leader on the issue of alcohol poisoning among youth. Mothers Against Drunk Driving (MADD) works actively with young people, many of whom voice their support of strong drinking-prevention programs for youth. Students Against Destructive Decisions (SADD) initiated a "2000x2000 Campaign" to reduce youth alcohol-related fatalities to 2,000 people by the end of the year 2000. Further information about these programs and what you can do to help can be obtained by contacting the organizations at the addresses on page 122. An increasing number of teens no longer consider driving while impaired acceptable.

• SEX AND ALCOHOL •

David was usually a gentle, considerate person, but Gina considered breaking up their relationship because his personality changed completely at parties. After he had a few drinks, she felt he had his hands all over her and was completely out of control. After each night of drinking he would promise that he would not treat her this way again, but he never kept his promise.

One night at a party, Gina decided to drink along with David. The evening ended with unplanned and unprotected sexual behavior, after which Gina decided to break her relationship with

David. The day after the incident, she was concerned that she might be pregnant. She did not consider the possibility of having contracted a sexually transmitted disease, even HIV, until long after the event.

Surveys suggest that alcohol use is associated with risky behavior and vulnerability to coercive sexual activity. In one study, 44 percent of sexually active Massachusetts teenagers said they were more likely to have sexual intercourse if they had been drinking, and 17 percent said they were less likely to use condoms after drinking.[17] This is not surprising since alcohol consumption is likely to lower inhibitions, to interfere with decision making and judgment, and to increase risk taking.

Drinking may actually lead to an increase in sexual assaults and risky sex. Men expect to feel more powerful, sexual, and aggressive after drinking alcohol. Studies show that men who think they have been drinking (whether they have or not) are more sexually aroused and are more responsive to erotic stimuli and rape scenarios.[18]

If a man starts out on a date thinking he is going to have sex, he may ignore his partner's protests. This has been called rape mentality. The majority of acquaintance rapes are planned in advance.

In many cases, alcohol is used to make partners more sexually willing than they would be otherwise. When women drink, they may miss cues that suggest a sexual assault. It may also decrease the likelihood that they can successfully resist one. Beth was feeling "mildly buzzed" when Joe persuaded her to go up to his bedroom. She didn't really want to go there, but she felt so relaxed that she did not resist. Joe decided she was fair game. If he was charged with rape afterward, he could say she had been willing to cooperate. Actually, Beth used bad judgment because of her drinking, but rape is always the responsibility of the rapist. Bad judgment is not a defense for rape.[19]

Numerous studies have shown that adolescents are more likely to engage in unprotected sex when they drink alcohol than when they do not.[20]

• FAMILY VIOLENCE •

Frequently, alcohol use or abuse can lead parents to become violent with their children. Many children whose parents drink heavily have learned to hide when mothers and/or fathers become violent. An estimated 30 percent of child-abuse cases may involve alcohol, and in many of these cases a mother, her live-in boyfriend, or a father suffers from alcoholism.[21]

A study of men charged with battering their partners found that 60 percent of them were under the influence of alcohol at the time of the incident.[22] Two-thirds of the violent-crime victims by a current or former spouse or boyfriend or girlfriend report that alcohol had been a factor. Alcohol is involved in 75 percent of spousal abuse.[23]

Many researchers have explored the relationship between alcohol and aggression using the following type of experiment: A person administers electric shocks to an unseen opponent both while sober and after consuming alcohol. The person is not told that the opponent is a computer that measures the amount of aggressiveness. In many studies, the person exhibited increased aggressiveness (by administering stronger shocks) in proportion to increasing alcohol consumption. However, the people giving the electric shocks rarely increased their aggression unless they felt threatened or provoked.[24]

Strong individual differences appear to be involved in the relationship between alcohol and violence. While most individuals experience heightened aggression with low doses and less aggression with high doses, some individuals experience reduced aggression with low doses of alcohol.

Violent behavior depends on a host of interacting factors, so there are no simple answers to the relationship between alcohol and violence. Much remains to be learned about this complex subject.[25]

• OTHER DANGEROUS BEHAVIOR •

Alcohol use is linked with many accidents that occur on or near water. Drownings, including those related to boating mishaps, are the third-leading cause of unintentional-injury deaths among all age groups. Alcohol is believed to be a major risk factor for drownings.[26] Drinking can increase the risk of death for boat operators as well as passengers. A drinking passenger may be at risk of falling overboard even when the boat is being driven safely or just drifting.

No one knows the exact number of diving accidents that have resulted in spinal injury, but alcohol involvement has been demonstrated in a large number of them. Someone who is drunk is less likely to check the depth of water in a pool or lake than someone who has not been drinking.

Alcohol may be a contributing factor in suicide, although no cause-and-effect relationship has been established. Research suggests several explanations for the high rate of alcohol use among suicide victims. Since alcohol may reduce inhibitions and impair judgment of someone contemplating suicide, it could make the act more likely. The use of alcohol may also aggravate other risk factors for suicide, such as depression, or other mental illness.

Alcohol also contributes to injuries and death from fires and burns. After a few drinks, sleepy persons who smoke cigarettes in bed have a high risk of setting the mattress and/or themselves on fire. Drinkers, awake or sleepy, may be unaware of small fires and even of smoke alarms in another part of the house until a fire is out of control.Drinking may affect the outcome of treatment for burn injuries. Studies show that fatality rates are higher among patients with high concentrations of blood alcohol compared with patients who have no measurable blood alcohol.[27]

Former Secretary of Health and Human Services Louis W. Sullivan has said that half of all injuries could be avoided by not drinking when you are driving, boating, operating machinery, feeling angry, or using a firearm.[28]

Chapter 10

Do You Have a Drinking Problem?

Many drinkers do not know whether or not they have a drinking problem. Even nondrinkers who think they know the truth about alcohol are not sure whether the following common statements are true. When you hear them, what do you believe?

- *"I can stop drinking any time. I just don't want to right now."*

This is one of the most common statements made by people who are having problems controlling the amount of alcohol they drink. Many of them really believe what they say. Alcoholism has been called a disease of denial.

- *"Your sex life will improve if you drink."*

A person may feel more suave and sexy after drinking, but chronic male alcoholics have reduced capacity for penile erection, decreased sperm production, and lower sperm counts. In some men, the testes may actually shrink. In extreme cases, a feminization syndrome may develop, which includes the development of breast tissue and loss of body hair.[1]

- *"I'll never be an alcoholic. I have built-in brakes. I can't drink too much because I get sick before I do."*

This does not protect against alcoholism. A person who drinks small amounts can become addicted. It does not matter entirely how much or how little one drinks. The important thing is how alcohol is affecting a person's life.

- *"I have a hollow leg. I can hold my liquor. Only sloppy drunks become alcoholics."*

Many people who are at risk for alcoholism have a high tolerance for alcohol. They can often drink large amounts without showing obvious impairment of the ability to walk, talk, and think. An alcoholic may be able to drink as much as a dozen beers or a liter of wine without acting drunk.

A typical nonalcoholic feels relaxed, euphoric, and energetic and can perform slightly better than normal with about an ounce of alcohol. With continued drinking, sedative effects cause behavior to deteriorate. An early alcoholic can show improved functioning, talk clearly, and walk a straight line with fairly high levels of alcohol, as long as drinking continues below the tolerance level. But when he or she stops drinking, performance deteriorates rapidly.

- *"I just started to drink a year ago, so I can't be an alcoholic. That takes years."*

Alcohol develops at different rates in different people. Some people become alcoholic very quickly, while others drink over a long period of time before becoming dependent on the drug. Definitions of alcoholism vary, and while some experts talk about teenage problem drinkers, most agree that there are many teenage alcoholics.

- *"The party was a real success, but most of us can't remember what happened."*

Many people who have blackouts, memory lapses of what happened when they were drunk the night before, think that this is a common experience. Most people who drink do not experience blackouts. Blackouts are rarely a reaction to social drinking. They are warning signs of alcoholism.

- *"Don't worry about me. I drink a lot but I'm not using drugs."*

The idea that alcohol is not a drug is widespread. Even many experts talk about alcohol *and* drug abuse, as if alcohol were not a drug. Perhaps they differentiate because alcohol is legal for people over 21, but alcohol is still a drug.

- *"I'm not an alcoholic! Do I look like a skid-row bum?"*

There is no typical alcoholic, although many people used to think of alcoholics as down-and-out homeless people. Alcoholics may be able to hide their problems for a while, but if they do not stop drinking, they will not be able to think clearly or maintain good physical health.

Alcoholism is incurable, although many alcoholics recover their health and career abilities by abstaining from drinking.

- *"Come on, a few drinks will make you feel better. I relax every day this way. It's a good way to stay healthy."*

Self-medication with alcohol is a dangerous way of relaxing. Exercise, listening to music, talking with friends, and a long list of other ways to relax are better medicine.

- *"It's rude to refuse a drink."*

It's rude to push people to drink. A simple "No thank you," is a polite answer.

- *"You won't get drunk if you stick to the same kind of drink. Switching drinks can be dangerous."*

- *"I never touch anything but beer. As long as I stay away from the hard stuff, I'll be OK."*

The alcohol in beer, wine, and liquor is the same. People who get drunk usually do so from drinking too much alcohol.

- *"If you are a child of an alcoholic, you will become one."*

Although you have a four to five times greater risk of becoming an alcoholic, most descendants of alcoholics do not develop the disease. The key to prevention is knowing when you are at risk and acting responsibly.

- *"You can always tell 'When to say when,' so it is safe to drive when you don't feel drunk."*

Although there are charts that show how drinking affects blood alcohol concentration, many factors are involved. Only two drinks can affect judgment. Drinking and driving don't mix, and if done by teenagers is against the law.

- *"I can't be an alcoholic because I haven't been arrested for drunk driving in five years."*

Some alcoholics have learned not to drive when they are drunk. They can make this statement without calling attention to the fact that they are alcoholics.

- *"Peggy fell into the cold water and is shivering. Get her a few beers to warm her up."*

Many people think that alcohol warms the body, perhaps because of old ideas based on pictures of dogs who carried small kegs of liquor to rescue freezing accident victims in the Swiss Alps. Peggy would be helped more by a cup of hot cocoa or whatever nonalcoholic beverage was available. Hot water would be far better than hot rum.

- *"If people can drive, vote, marry without parental consent before the age of 21, they should be able to drink, too."*

Although it may seem logical to grant all adult privileges at the same age, some privileges carry greater responsibilities and risks to others. If someone makes a mistake about whom to marry, that mainly affects the couple. If someone votes for the wrong person, not much harm is done. When people drink irresponsibly, they become a serious life threat to themselves and to other members of society.[2]

- *"I'd like to stop drinking, but I cannot afford treatment."*

Alcoholics Anonymous is free.

- *"If I pour my father's gin down the sink and hide all the other alcohol in the house, he will have to stop drinking."*

Alcoholics cannot be forced into treatment by pouring their supply down the sink or removing alcohol from the house. A person must be willing to go for treatment.

Some alcoholics who cannot obtain beverage alcohol crave it so much that they drink disinfectant for its alcohol content.

- *"Drunks stay drunk."*

Most people drink more heavily on weekends and start out each day alcohol-free.

- *"Alcoholics have psychiatric problems that they attempt to medicate with alcohol."*

About 20 percent of alcoholics suffer from a psychiatric disorder such as depression and anxiety. Many times these problems are caused by drinking and disappear when the drinkers stop.[3]

- *"Alcoholics drink because their friends do."*

When people drink heavily, their friends who do not drink or drink moderately tend to fall away, leaving a peer group that consists mostly of alcoholics.

- *"I need to drink to be accepted."*

The use of alcohol often results in people becoming less accepted, not more accepted, because behavior under the influence can make them the object of humor, ridicule, or disgust. The abuse of alcohol can have serious negative effects on relationships of all kinds.

- *"Alcohol gives me energy."*

Alcohol is a depressant. It slows down your ability to speak, think, and move.

- *"It's no one's business if I drink too much."*

All people who drink too much have some relatives or friends who worry about them. If they drive, they endanger the lives of others. According to MADD, each of the 12 million problem drinkers in the United States affects four other people.[4]

NOTES

CHAPTER ONE

1. Hayley R. Mitchell, *Teen Alcoholism.* San Diego: Lucent Books, 1998, p. 6.

2. http://www.cspinet.org/booze/drugwar.htm

3. Bert L. Valee, "Alcohol in the Western World," *Scientific American,* June 1998, p. 85

4. Ibid.

5. http://www.cspinet.org/booze/bzn_0898/massing.htm

CHAPTER TWO

1. Karen Bellenir, editor, *Substance Abuse Sourcebook.* Detroit: Omnigraphics, 1996, pp. 199–212.

2. Ibid., p. 205.

3. Ibid., p. 207.

4. Ibid., p. 208.

5. "School Spreads Alcohol Policy to Wine Sips in Paris," *New York Times,* May 31, 1998.

6. "States Seek to Curb Mail Order Alcohol," *Christian Science Monitor,* November 25, 1997.

7. InfoActive Health, "Alcohol and Tobacco on the Web: Sites are Still Hazardous to Your Children's Health,"

Washington, D.C.: Center for Media Education, 1998, pp. 3–4.

8. Wendy Williams and others, "Alcohol and Tobacco on the Web: New Threats to Youth," A Report by the Center for Media Education, Washington, D.C.: Center for Media Education, 1997, p. 1.

9. InfoActive Health, p. 2.

10. Center for Science in the Public Interest, "Rep. Kennedy Lauded for Six-Pack Approach to Alcohol Advertising," Press Release, May 16, 1996.

11. http://www.cspinet.org/booze/drugwar.htm

12. Laurie Leiber, "A Pilot Study to Assess Beer Commercial Recall by Children Age 9 to 11 Years," Berkeley, CA: Center on Alcohol Advertising, May 1996, Abstract, p. 1.

13. George Hacker, Statement, CASA Adolescent Commission Report, Alcohol Policies Project, August 13, 1997, p. 1.

14. http://www.cspinet.org/booze/f_liq_ad.htm

15. "MADD Tackles Alcohol Marketers for Super Bowl Ads Appealing to Youth," Dallas: MADD Press Release, January 22, 1998.

16. http://www.marininstitute.org/phatletter/html

17. http://www.cspinet.org/booze/f_liq_ad.htm

18. "Nationwide Poll Reveals Viewers Want TV Airwaves Dry," Michigan State University Media Communications, February 4, 1998.

CHAPTER THREE

1. Karen Bellenir, editor, *Substance Abuse Sourcebook.* Detroit: Omnigraphics, 1996, p. 205.

2. Ibid. p. 203.

3. Darryl S. Inaba and others, *Uppers, Downers and All Arounders.* Ashland, OR: CNS Publications, 1997, p. 182.

CHAPTER FOUR

1. "California Joins Movement to Restrict Teenage Driving," *Christian Science Monitor*, July 3, 1998.

2. Karen Bellenir, editor, *Substance Abuse Sourcebook*. Detroit: Omnigraphics, 1996, p. 205.

3. http://www.madd.org/stats/stat_youth.shtml

4. http://www.cspinet.org/booze/alcyouth.html, p. 1.

5. http://www.glness.com/ndhs/stats.html, p. 1.

6. Thomas P. Gullotta and others, *Substance Misuse in Adolescence*. Thousand Oaks, CA: Sage, 1995, p. 3.

7. Susan and Daniel Cohen, *A Six-Pack and a Fake ID*. New York: M. Evans, 1986, p. 97.

8. P. J. Cook and G. Tauchen, "The Effects of Minimum Drinking Age Legislation on Youthful Auto Fatalities, 1970–1977," *Journal of Legal Studies*, 1984, pp. 159-162.

9. D. A. Maisto and J. V. Rachal, *Minimum-Drinking-Age Laws*, Lexington, MA: D.C. Heath, 1980, pp. 155–176.

10. http://www.pathfinder.com/alt.culture p.1

11. Ruth C. Engs, "Why the Drinking Age Should Be Lowered: An Opinion Based upon Research." Bloomington, IN: Opinion Paper, 1998, p. 1.

12. Ibid., p. 2.

13. http://www.scpinet,org/booze/mlpatalk.htm

14. Bridget F. Grant, National Institute on Alcohol Abuse and Alcoholism, at press conference on the age of onset of alcohol abuse, Washington, D.C., January 14, 1998.

15. Henry Wechsler and others, "Enforcing the Minimum Drinking Age Law: A Survey of College Administrators and Security Chiefs." Newton, MA: The Higher Education Center for Alcohol and Other Drug Prevention, 1993, p. 9.

16. Jim Hall, Chairman, National Transportation Safety Board, at press conferences on the National Drunk and Drugged Driving Prevention Month, Washington, D.C., December 18, 1997.

17. New York State Office of Alcoholism and Substance Abuse Service, "Minimum Legal Purchase Age and Safety Traffic Safety: Facts and Practices," January 1997.

18. Ibid.

19. http://www.cspinet.org/booze/mlpafact.htm, 1998.

20. NIAAA News Release, January 14, 1998, p. 1.

21. "Young Drinkers More Likely to Become Alcoholics," *MADD News*, January 15, 1998, p. 1.

22. "Kids Quickly Build Tolerance to Alcohol," as reported by Associated Press, March 20, 1998.

23. Cynthia Kuhn and others, *Buzzed: The Straight Facts About the Most Used and Abused Drugs.* New York: Norton, 1998, pp. 59–60.

CHAPTER FIVE

1. http://h-devil.www.mc.duke.edu/h-devil/drugs/alcohol.htm

2. Daryl S. Inaba and others, *Uppers, Downers and All Arounders.* Ashland, OR: CNS Publications, 1997, p. 184.

3. http://www.jointogether.org/sa/wire/news/reader.jtml?Object_ID=25126

4. Cynthia Kuhn and others, *Buzzed.* New York: W. W. Norton, 1998, p. 33.

5. Ibid., p. 33.

6. Alcohol Alert #35, 1997, p. 1.

7. Kuhn, p. 29.

8. Bureau of Justice Statistics, "Alcohol and Crime," Washington, D.C., U.S. Department of Justice, 1998, p. v.

9. Secretary of Health and Human Services, *Alcohol and Health*, Ninth Special Report to Congress, 1997, pp. 145-146.

10. http://www.cspinet.org/booze/198bzn.htm, p. 3.

11. http://silk.nih.gov/silk/niaaal/questions/q-a.htm#question17

12. Alcohol Alert #27, Bethesda, MD: National Institute of Alcohol Abuse and Alcoholism, 1995, p. 1.

13. Ibid., p. 2.

14. Ibid., p. 2.

15. Marilyn Webb, *The Good Death.* New York: Bantam Books, 1997, p. 127.

16. Kuhn, p. 52.

17. Alcohol Alert #27, p. 4.

18. Tufts University, *Health and Nutrition Letter*, January 1998, p. 2.

19. Ibid., p. 4.

CHAPTER SIX

1. Michael Dorris, *The Broken Cord.* New York: Harper & Row, 1989.

2. Phillip W. Long, "Fetal Alcohol Syndrome." *The Harvard Mental Health Letter*: November 1990.
http://www.mentalhealth.com/mag1/p5h-fas 1.html

3. P. Lemoine, & coauthors, "Children of Alcoholic Parents: Anomalies Observed in 127 Cases." *Oest Med* 1968, vol. 21, pp. 476-482.

4. Alcohol use in pregnancy on the rise. *InteliHealth.* August 3, 1998.
http://www.intelihealth.com

5. Phillip W. Long, "Fetal Alcohol Syndrome." *The Harvard Mental Health Letter*: November 1990.
http://www.mentalhealth.com/mag 1/p5h-fas 1.html

6. http://www.intelihealth.com

7. C. Larkby and N. Day, "The Effects of Prenatal Alcohol Exposure," *Alcohol Health and Research World* 1997, vol. 21, p. 192.

8. Effects of Alcohol on Fetal and Postnatal Development, *Ninth Special Report to the U.S. Congress on Alcohol and Health.* National Institute on Alcohol Abuse and Alcoholism, Bethesda, MD, 1997, p.193.

9. Identification of Children with Fetal Alcohol Syndrome and Opportunity for Referral of Their Mothers for Primary Prevention, Washington, D.C. 1993-1997, *Morbidity and Mortality Weekly Report.* Centers for Disease Control and Prevention, U.S. Department of Health and Human Services, October 16, 1998, vol. 47, p. 861.

10. M. Carrington Reid, M.D., personal communication, October 1998.

CHAPTER SEVEN

1. http://www.udel.edu/PR/Update/98/9/unite/html

2. http://www.health.org/pubs/lastcall/chapter1.htm, p. 6

3. Rob Foss, Research Scientist, UNC Highway Safety Research Center, Personal Communication, August 20, 1998.

4. NIAAA, Alcohol Alert, #37, July 1997, p 1.

5. http://www.hsph.harvard.edu/press/releases/press91098.html

6. Ibid.

7. "Bellying Up to the Bar," *Newsweek*, September 21, 1998, p. 89.

8. http://www.health.org/pubs/primer/binge.htm, p. 1.

9. Henry Wechsler, "Last Call," *Harvard School of Public Health Alcohol Study*, Rockville, MD: NCADI, Preface, 1997.

10. William DeJong, *Preventing Alcohol-Related Problems on Campus*. Newton, MA: Higher Education Center for Alcohol and Other Drug Prevention, p. 9.

11. Ibid., p. 12.

12. http://www.cspinet.org/booze/alcyouth.html

13. "A Drinking Death Rattles Elite MIT," *New York Times*, October 1, 1997.

14. NCADI, "Binge Drinking Continues on College Campuses." Rockville, MD: *Prevention Alert*, Volume 1, No. 9, 1997, p. 1

15. Jon B. Bishop, "Binge Drinking on College Campuses: A New Approach to an Old Problem," University of Delaware: *Curbing High Risk Drinking*, 1998, p. 2.

16. Wechsler, "Last Call," Chapter I, p. 2.

17. "Colleges Turn to Peer Pressure to Curb Drinking," *Christian Science Monitor*, October 27, 1997.

18. Marc Clayton, "Dry Housing Grows Even as Students Protest Alcohol Bans," *Christian Science Monitor*, May 12, 1998.

19. "Bellying up to the Bar," *Newsweek*, September 21, 1998, p. 89.

20. "Fraternity Leaders Appear to Be the First in Line for Alcohol," *New York Times*, December 15, 1997.

21. "Plugging the Kegs," *U.S. News & World Report*, January 26, 1998, p. 67.

22. Jon Garfunkel, "Abolishing Fraternities Isn't the Answer to Drinking," *New York Times*, October 7, 1997.

23. "A Collective Wallop Against Alcohol Abuse on Campus," *Christian Science Monitor*, December 11, 1998, pp. 2-3.

CHAPTER EIGHT

1. Ronald L. Rogers and C. Scott McMillen, *Alcoholism: Reducing Your Risk*. New York: Bantam Books, pp. 14–15 and back cover.

2. "Curbing the Urge to Drink," *New York Times*, July 31, 1998.

3. National Institute on Alcohol Abuse and Alcoholism, "Frequently Asked Questions," http://www.niaaa.nih.org

4. Herbert Fingarette, "We Should Reject the Disease Concept of Alcoholism," *Harvard Mental Health Newsletter*, February 1990, pp.2-3.

5. Darryl S. Inaba and others, *Uppers, Downers, and All Arounders.* Ashland, OR: CNS Publications, 1997, p. 210.

6. Ibid., p. 69.

7. Ibid., pp. 72–73.

8. http://www.parentsplace.com/readroom/aacap/alcoholc.html

9. Michael Windle, "Concepts and Issues in COA Research," Washington, D.C: *Alcohol and Health Research World*, Vol. 21, Number 3, p. 186.

10. Jane Claypool, *Alcohol and You.* Danbury, CT: Franklin Watts, 1997, p. 18.

11. "Curbing the Urge to Drink," *New York Times*, July 31, 1998.

Chapter Nine

1. "Alcohol Alert #38," NIAAA, 1997, p. 1.

2. "Alcohol or Drug Link Seen in 80 percent of Jailings," *New York Times*, January 9, 1998.

3. Lawrence Greenfeld, "Alcohol and Crime," Washington, D.C.: U.S. Department of Justice, 1998, p.3.

4. William J. Bennett and others, *Body Count.* New York: Simon & Schuster, 1996, p.67.

5. "Deaths Due to Alcohol," *Scientific American*," December 1996, pp. 30-31.

6. E. Gluksman, "Alcohol and Alcohol Problems," *British Medical Bulletin*, Vol. 50, Number 2, 1994, pp. 76–84.

7. "15-Year-Old Girl Pleads Guilty to Manslaughter in Central Park Killing," *New York Times*, March 12, 1998.

8. "Deadly End to a Dangerous Game," *Boston Globe*, March 18, 1997.

9. "Police and UConn Students Trade Charges After Weekend Melee," *New York Times*, April 28, 1998.

10. http://www.nhtsa.dot.gov

11. http://www.csaa.com/education/smart/drkdvfcts

12. http://www/nhtsa.dot.gov

13. InteliHealth, "Alcohol a Major Factor in Bicycling Injuries and Death," Johns Hopkins Press Release, January 27, 1997.

14. http://www.hwysafety.org/qanda/qaalgnrl.htm

15. Ibid.

16. "Looking for Someone to Blame," *Newsweek*, September 15, 1997, p. 49.

17. L. Strunin and R. Hingtson, "Alcohol, Drugs, and Adolescent Behavior," *International Journal of the Addictions*, 27 (2): p.129–146, 1992.

18. http://www2.bitstream.net/~alpropes/resc/alcohol.html

19. Ibid.

20. Ninth Special Report to the U.S. Congress on Alcohol and Health, p. 266.

21. Ibid., p. 262.

22. Ibid., p. 262.

23. http://www.cspinet.org/booze/bzn_0898/crime.htm

24. Alcohol Alert #38, p. 2.

25. Albert J. Reis, Jr. and Jeffrey A. Roth, editors, *Understanding and Preventing Violence*. Washington, D.C.: National Academy Press, p. 189, 211.

26. Ninth Special Report, p. 254.

27. Ibid. p. 268.

28. http://www.miph.org/fs4.html

Chapter Ten

1. Cynthia Kuhn and others, *Buzzed*. New York: W. W. Norton, 1997, pp. 48–49.

2. Bob Foss, *What Is the Right Drinking Age?* Chapel Hill: University of North Carolina, March 1998, p. 2.

3. Joanne Ellison Rodgers, "Addiction: A Whole New View," *Psychology Today*, p. 49.

4. Under 21, "Some Myths About Alcohol," MADD, Dallas, TX: MADD Programs Department, 1998, pp. 2–3.

SUGGESTED READING

Barbour, Scott, editor, *Alcohol: Opposing Viewpoints.* Greenhaven Press, 1997.

Claypool, Jane, *Alcohol and You.* Danbury, CT: Franklin Watts, 1997.

Cohen, Daniel, *Prohibition: America Makes Alcohol Illegal.* Brookfield, CT: The Millbrook Press, 1995.

Harris, Jonathan, *This Drinking Nation.* New York: Simon & Schuster, 1994.

Hyde, Margaret O., *Alcohol: Uses and Abuses.* Hillside, NJ: Enslow, 1988.

Inaba, Darryl, William E. Cohen and Michael E. Holstein, *Uppers, Downers, and All Arounders.* Ashland, OR: CNS Publications, 1997.

Kuhn, Cynthia, Scott Swartwelder, and Wilkie Wilson, *Buzzed: The Straight Facts About Most Used and Abused Drugs.* New York: W. W. Norton, 1998.

Lender, Mark Edward, *Drinking in America: A History.* New York: The Free Press, 1982.

Mitchell, Hayley R., *Teen Alcoholism.* San Diego: Lucent Books, 1998.

Pringle, Laurence, *Drinking.* New York: Morrow, 1997.

Rogers, Ronald L. and C. Scott McMillen, *Alcoholism: Reducing Your Risk.* New York: Bantam Books, 1992.

Rublowsky, John, *The Stoned Age: A History of Drugs in America.* New York: Putnam, 1974.

GLOSSARY

abstinence: choosing not to participate in a certain behavior, such as refraining from drinking alcohol.

abuse: the misuse of a substance or behavior.

addiction: repetitive compulsive use of a substance that occurs despite negative consequences to the user; a strong physical or psychological need for a drug.

AIDS: acquired immunodeficiency syndrome, an incurable and fatal disease of the body's immune system.

Al-Anon: a worldwide organization for spouses or other relatives and friends of alcoholics.

Al-Ateen: an organization for children of alcoholics.

alcohol abuse: excessive use of alcohol; differs from alcoholism by not including an extremely strong craving for alcohol, loss of control, or physical dependence.

Alcoholics Anonymous (AA): a worldwide organization of recovering alcoholics.

alcoholism: a condition in which a person has become addicted to alcohol and continues its use despite harmful consequences.

antabuse: (disulfiram) a medication used to help people remain sober.

binge drinking: often defined as drinking four or more drinks on one occasion for women, five or more drinks for men.

Some alcohol researchers prefer to define binge drinking as uncontrolled drinking for two days.

blackout: being unable to remember what was said or what happened when one was drunk. Occurs after a person is sober, often "the morning after."

blood alcohol concentration: the percentage of alcohol in the blood; often called BAC.

booze: any alcoholic beverage.

breathalyzer: a device used to measure blood alcohol concentration by measuring the breath.

chronic: recurring or continuing for long periods of time.

cirrhosis: a liver disease in which tissue becomes scarred and damaged by alcohol abuse; nutrients cannot be processed normally.

delirium tremens (DTs): trembling, nausea, insomnia, and hallucinations caused by sudden withdrawal from alcohol in someone addicted to it; medical help is needed.

dependence: need for a drug.

depressant: a drug that slows down mental and bodily functions. Alcohol is a depressant; often called a downer.

distillation: heating wine or beer to turn alcohol into a gas; this gas is then cooled and becomes liquid alcohol, or distilled spirits.

drug: a chemical that changes the way a person thinks, feels, or acts.

drunk: the way people feel and act when they have consumed enough alcohol to cause them to lose most or all control of their actions and thoughts; same as intoxicated.

ethyl alcohol: the kind of alcohol used in beverages. At low doses, such as one or two drinks, it acts as a stimulant. At higher doses it is a depressant.

fermentation: the action of yeast on the sugar in fruit juices or cereals to produce alcohol, which can be used to make beverages such as beer and wine.

fetal alcohol syndrome: a group of symptoms that may affect an unborn child when the pregnant mother drinks alcohol. Negative effects include birth defects, mental retardation, and other problems.

hallucination: seeing or hearing something that is not actually present.

hangover: physical effects after heavy drinking, when alcohol has left the body; usually includes headache, nausea, and fatigue.

hepatitis: inflamed liver disease that may be caused by prolonged, heavy drinking.

inhibition: restraining behavior; alcohol releases inhibitions.

intoxication: bodily changes brought on by a drug. Comes from the word "toxin," which means poison. Usually involves changes in thought process and loss of control over normal functions.

metabolism: the building up and breaking down of tissue.

naltrexone (ReVia): a medication used to treat alcoholism.

overdose: a dangerously high amount of a drug, which can cause serious health problems, even death.

peer: a person of the same age and social position. Peer pressure happens when people with no special authority try to get other people like them to do or not do something.

predisposition: being susceptible to something; being more likely than others to develop something, such as a disease.

prohibition: the era between 1920 and 1933 when it was illegal to buy, sell, manufacture, or transport any alcoholic beverage within the United States and its territories.

relapse: the return of a person in a treatment program to drinking.

social drinker: a person who drinks alcohol but does not drink enough to cause any problems, usually limited to one or two drinks per day.

sting operation: an undercover police operation.

withdrawal: the process of eliminating a drug from the body; usually involves vomiting and chills (see delirium tremens). Psychological healing may take months or even years.

FOR FURTHER INFORMATION

Al-Anon and Al-Ateen
1600 Corporate Landing Parkway
Virginia Beach, VA 23454
804-563-1600
http://al-anon.alateen.org
Meeting information- 1-800-344-2666

Alcoholics Anonymous (AA)
P.O. Box 459, Grand Central Station
New York, NY 10163
http://www.aa.org
See local phone book for meetings
Meetings on the Web: http://stayingcyber.org

Center for Media Education
Telecommunications Policy in the Public Interest
1511 K Street, NW, #518
Washington, DC 20005
202-332-9110
http://tap.epn.org/cme

Center for Science in the Public Interest
1875 Connecticut Avenue
· Washington, DC 20009-5278
202-332-9110, Extension 385
Email: alcproject@cspinet.org
http://www.cspinet.org/booze

Center on Addiction and Substance Abuse at Columbia University (CASA)
1301 Avenue of the Americas
New York, NY 10019-6092
212-259-8600
http://www.casacolumbia.org

Center on Alcohol Advertising
2140 Shattuck Avenue, #1201
Berkeley, CA 94704
510-649-8970
http://www.traumafdn.org/alcohol/ads/index.html
Email: Lleiber@traumafdn.org

Children of Alcoholics Foundation
33 West 60th Street
New York, NY 10023
212-757-2100, Extension 6370
Email: coaf@phoenixhouse.org

Do It Now Foundation
P.O. Box 27548
Tempe, AZ 85285
602-491-0393
http://www.doitnow.org

Join Together
441 Stuart Street, 6th Floor
Boston, MA 02116
617-437-1500
http://www.jointogether.com

Marin Institute for the Prevention of Alcohol
and Other Drug Problems
24 Belvedere Street
San Rafael, CA 94901
http:www.marininstitute.org

Mothers Against Drunk Driving (MADD)
P.O. Box 541688
Dallas, TX 75354
http://www.MADD.org/

National Association for Native American
Children of Alcoholics
611 12th Avenue South, Suite 200
Seattle, WA 98144
800-322-5601

National Black Child Development Institute
463 Rhode Island Avenue NW
Washington, DC 20005
800-556-2234

National Clearinghouse for Alcohol and
  Drug Information
(NCADI)
P.O. Box 2345
Rockville, MD 20852
301-468-2600
800-729-6686
http://www.health.org

National Council on Alcoholism and
  Drug Dependence, Inc.
12 West 21st Street
New York, NY 10010
800-NCA-CALL
http://www.ncadd.org

National Institute on Alcohol Abuse and Alcoholism
P.O. Box 10686
Rockville, MD 20849-0686
http://www.niaaa.nih.gov

National Institute on Drug Abuse
5600 Fishers Lane
Rockville, MD 20857
National toll free hotline:
1-800-662-HELP

Remove Intoxicated Drivers (RID)
P.O. BOX 520
Schenectady, NY 12301
510-372-0034

Students Against Destructive Decisions (SADD)
P.O. Box 800
Marlboro, MA 01752
508-481-5759

Women for Sobriety
P.O. Box 618
Quakertown, PA 18951
1-800-333-1606

INDEX

abstinence, 59, 60
acamprosate (Campral), 85
acetaldehyde, 42
acetaminophen (Tylenol),
  47, 48
addiction, 75
advertising alcohol, 18-23
aggression, alcohol and,
  87-88, 95-96
Al-Anon, 81
Al-Ateen, 81-83
alcohol (see also alco-
  holism, binge drinking)
    absorption rate, 41
    advertising, 18-23
    aggression and, 87-88,
      95-96
    amount consumed, 31-
      32
    attitudes towards, 14
    availability of, 17-18
    basic facts about, 9-11
    beer (see beer)
    brain and, 36, 39, 40,
      54-55
    common statements
      about, 98-103
    crime and, 87-88

depressant effects of,
  43, 103
distilled spirits (hard
  liquor), 28
drownings and, 96
eliminating from body,
  41-42
family violence and,
  95-96
gender and effects of,
  39-40
health benefits of, 43-
  44
home delivery of, 18
media messages about,
  13
median age at starting
  to drink, 30
medication interac-
  tions, 45-48
parents, messages
  from, 14-17
physical effects of, 38-
  40
pregnancy and, 50-53
sexual activity and, 39,
  93-95
suicide and, 97

tolerance to, 36, 41, 98
wine (see wine)
withdrawal symptoms,
43, 75, 76-77
alcohol abuse, defined, 75
alcohol education efforts,
60
alcohol-free dorms and
activities, 65, 68
Alcoholics Anonymous
(AA), 74, 81, 84, 86, 101
alcoholism, 71-86 (see also
alcohol)
age of drinking onset
and, 33-34
case studies of, 71-74
children of alcoholics,
79-81
defined, 74-75, 100
elderly and, 57-58
fetal alcohol syndrome
and, 50-53
genetics and, 78-79
incidence of, 75
medical effects of, 54-
57
research on, 78-79
risks for, 78
symptoms of, 74-75
theories of, 77
treatment of, 81, 84-86
withdrawal symptoms,
43, 75, 76-77
ales, 25
anemia, 56
antibiotics, 45
antidepressants, 45
antihistamines, 48
aspirin, 47
automobile accidents,
alcohol-related, 15, 22,
29-33, 89-93, 101-102

beer, 14
advertising, 18-23
brewing, 25
high-school-student
drinking, 26
ingredients in, 24-25
keg registration, 67-68
varieties of, 25, 26
bicycle injuries and deaths,
90
bile, 55-56
binge drinking, 13, 59-70
age of onset of, 61
approaches to curbing,
68-70
confronting, 64-66
death resulting from,
62-63
defined, 30, 60
fraternities/sororities
and, 66-68
incidence of, 60
reasons for, 61-62
blackouts, 78, 100
blood alcohol concentra-
tion (BAC), 15, 40, 90-92,
97, 101
blood pressure, 45, 46, 56,
57
body weight, 40, 42
Boost Alcohol Awareness
Concerning University
Students (BACCUS),
68, 69
booze, defined, 11
bourbon, 28
brain, alcohol and, 36, 39,
54-55
brandy, 28
breast cancer, 44
breast-feeding, 52
Breathalyzer test, 42, 90

Budweiser beer, 18, 20

cancer, 44, 56
carbohydrates, 24
cardiovascular disease, 44
celebration drinking (occasion), 11, 30, 88-89
Center for Media Education (CME), 19
Center for Science in the Public Interest, 21
Center for Substance Abuse Prevention (CASP), 30
Center on Alcohol Advertising, 21, 22
cerebellum, 55
cerebral hemorrhage, 57
child abuse, 94
children of alcoholics, 79-81
Children of Alcoholics Foundation, 81
cholesterol, 45, 56
circulatory system, 56
cirrhosis, 55-56
congeners, 41
Connecticut Coalition to Stop Underage Drinking, 16
cordials, 28
coronary heart disease, 44
corpus callosum, 55
craving, 75, 103
crime, alcohol and, 87-88

Darvon, 47
delirium tremens (DTs), 54, 76
depressant effects of alcohol, 43, 103

designated driver programs, 33
Dilantin, 47
distilled spirits (hard liquor), 28
Distilled Spirits Council of the United States (DISCUS), 21
disulfiram (Antabuse), 85
draft, 29, 31, 32
drinking age, 14, 29-37
drownings, 96
drunk driving, 15, 22, 29-33, 89-93, 101-102
DUI (driving under the influence) arrests, 35
Duke University Medical Center, 36

Education, Department of, 14
elderly, alcoholism and, 57-58
Engs, Ruth C., 33, 34
esophageal cancer, 56
ethyl alcohol, 11, 24

fake IDs, 17
family violence, 94-95
Federal Trade Commission, 22
fermentation, 24, 25, 27
fetal alcohol syndrome (FAS), 50-53
fraternities, alcohol and, 66-68
frontal lobe, 38
funneling, 66

gastritis, 56
gender, effects of alcohol and, 39-40

genetics, alcoholism and, 78-79
gin, 28
Gordis, Enoch, 35, 48

Hacker, George, 20
Hall, Jim, 34
hallucinations, 54, 76
hangovers, 42, 76
Harvard School of Public Health College Alcohol Study, 60
HDL cholesterol, 44
Health and Human Services, Department of, 30
health benefits of alcohol, 43-44
heart, alcohol and, 56-57
heart disease, 44, 45
Heath, Dwight, 15
hepatitis, 55
HIV infection, 73, 93
holiday heart syndrome, 56
home delivery of alcohol, 18
hops, 25
hybrid beers, 25

ibuprofen (Advil), 47
identification (ID), 17
information sources, 119-122
Internet
    advertising alcohol on, 18, 19
    ordering alcohol on, 18
Irish whiskey, 28

Johnston, Lloyd, 61

ketoprofen (Actron and Orudis KT), 47

Korsakoff's psychosis, 55
Krueger, Scott, 63

lagers, 25
legal drinking age, 14, 29-37
liqueurs, 28
liver, 42, 45, 55-56
liver cancer, 56
liver transplant, 56
Louisiana State University, 63

Madeira, 27
mail-order industry, 18
malt, 25
malt liquor, 25
Marin Institute, 21
mash, 25
medical effects of alcoholism, 54-57
medication-alcohol inter-actions, 45, 47-48
memory, 54, 55, 78, 100
metabolism, 42, 46
Michigan State University, 22
Mill, John Stuart, 29
MIT (Massachusetts Institute of Technology), 63
Mothers Against Drunk Driving (MADD), 21, 92, 120
mouth cancer, 56
Mullen, Tommy, 88

naltrexone (ReVia), 85
naproxen sodium (Aleve), 47
narcotics, 45, 47
National Association of Children of Alcoholics, 81

National Center on
  Addiction and
  Substance Abuse
  (CASA), Alcohol
  Policies Project of, 20
National Institute on
  Alcohol Abuse and
  Alcoholism (NIAAA),
  74
National Interfraternity
  Council, 67
National Panhellenic
  Conference, 68
National Study of
  Adolescent Drinking
  Behavior, 32
Nunnallee, Karolyn, 21

oxidation, 41, 42

pancreas, 56
party time, 88-89
peer pressure, 16, 17, 65, 77
Phat Boy Malt Liquor, 21
polyneuropathy, 55
port, 27
porter, 25, 26
pregnancy, alcohol and, 50-
  53
Prohibition, 31

Quinlan, Karen Ann, 47

rape, 93-95
Reid, M. Carrington, 57
relapse, 85
Remove Intoxicated
  Drivers (RID), 92
rum, 28
rye, 28

Schwarzbeck, Charles, 40
Scotch, 28

sedatives, 45, 48, 76
sexual activity, 39, 40,
  93-95
sherry, 27
sleep problems, 54
social drinkers, 43-44
social ostracism, 36
sororities, 66-68
sparkling wines, 27
specialty beers, 25
spousal abuse, 95
sting operations, 17-18
stout, 25, 26
Students Against Drunk
  Driving (SADD), 68-69,
  93
substance-free dorms, 65
sugars, 24
suicide, alcohol and, 97
Sullivan, Louis W., 97

television advertising, 20-
  22
testosterone, 39
throat cancer, 56
tolerance, 36, 42, 75, 98
Transportation,
  Department of, 15
tryamine, 45
twin studies, 78

University of Connecticut
  at Storrs, 89
University of Delaware,
  64
University of Michigan, 65
University of Minnesota,
  Alcohol Epidemiology
  Program of, 18
unprotected sex, 73, 93-94

Valee, Bert L., 10
Vietnam war, 32

vitamin deficiencies, 55
vodka, 28
voting age, 29, 31, 32

Wechsler, Henry, 60
whiskey, 28
wine
    color of, 26
    coolers, 14, 27

making, 27
    sparkling, 27
withdrawal symptoms, 43,
    75, 76-77
Wynne, Benjamin, 63

yeast, 24, 25, 27

zero-tolerance laws, 15, 91